"What is the difference between striving for excellence and seeking perfection? The former is attainable, the latter is not. The former spurs us on, the latter so often leads to chronic frustration, even despair and depression. "In *Perfecting Ourselves to Death* Dr. Winter ably explores this apparent paradox and charts the emergence of perfectionism with its varied origins in our genetic inheritance, upbringing, temperament and motivation.

"As a teacher and counselor, he combines a background of medicine and psychiatry along with a clear biblical foundation and many years of pastoral experience. The result is a book which is thoughtful, clear and accessible and will provide an invaluable practical resource for preachers, counselors and sufferers alike."

MONTY BARKER, CONSULTANT PSYCHIATRIST AND VISITING PROFESSOR OF PSYCHIATRY AND PASTORAL CARE

"Somewhere in each of us there is always a voice that says, 'Not yet have you done enough.' Richard Winter helps us identify the source of the voice, whether it echoes from ancient caverns of parental criticism, the packaged idealisms of pop culture or the streams of doubt flowing from a damaged soul. Then he surprises us by showing that the echoes cannot come from everywhere if they are not true. The joy of this wonderful book is not its denial of the truths of our perfectionism but the writer's delight in the greater truths that drown the echoes of our self-doubt in a voice of love far greater."

BRYAN CHAPPELL, PRESIDENT, COVENANT THEOLOGICAL SEMINARY

"Here is a clinically competent discipling resource that has been written to help Christians see how dehumanizing perfectionism spoils lives and to show how it may be overcome in Christ. To the other-oriented perfectionists, self-oriented perfectionists and other frazzled folk whom Professor Winter addresses he shows himself a truly wise guide."

J. I. PACKER, BOARD OF GOVERNORS PROFESSOR OF THEOLOGY, REGENT COLLEGE

PERFECTING OURSELVES TO DEATH

The Pursuit of Excellence and the Perils of Perfectionism

Richard Winter

IVP Books

An imprint of InterVarsity Press
Downers Grove, Illinois

InterVarsity Press
P.O. Box 1400, Downers Grove, IL 60515-1426
World Wide Web: www.ivpress.com
E-mail: email@ivpress.com

InterVarsity Press® is the book-publishing division of InterVarsity Christian Fellowship/USA®, a student movement active on campus at hundreds of universities, colleges and schools of nursing in the United States of America, and a member movement of the International Fellowship of Evangelical Students. For information about local and regional activities, write Public Relations Dept., InterVarsity Christian Fellowship/USA, 6400 Schroeder Rd., P.O. Box 7895, Madison, WI 53707-7895, or visit the IVCF website at <www.intervarsity.org>.

All Scripture quotations, unless otherwise indicated, are taken from the Holy Bible, New International Version®. NIV®. Copyright ©1973, 1978, 1984 by International Bible Society. Used by permission of Zondervan Publishing House. All rights reserved.

Design: Cindy Kiple

Images: Four 10 scores: Michael Coqliantry/Getty Images
 Smug and unsure expressions: Ryan McVay/Getty Images
 Cool guy and surprised expression: Mark Andersen/Getty Images

ISBN 978-0-8308-3259-0

Printed in the United States of America ∞

Library of Congress Cataloging-in-Publication Data

Winter, Richard, 1945-
 Perfecting ourselves to death: the pursuit of excellence and the
 perils of perfectionism / Richard Winter.
  p. cm.
 Includes bibliographical references.
 ISBN 0-8308-3259-9 (pbk.: alk paper)
 1. Perfectionism (Personality trait)—Religious
aspects—Christianity. 2. Excellence—Religious
aspects—Christianity. I. Title
BV4597.58.P47W56 2005
241'.4—dc22

                                                                    2004029845

| P | 21 | 20 | 19 | 18 | 17 | 16 | 15 | 14 | 13 | 12 | 11 | 10 | 9 | 8 | 7 |
| Y | 23 | 22 | 21 | 20 | 19 | 18 | 17 | 16 | 15 | 14 | 13 | 12 | | | |

To Jane, who loves me well—

my dearest friend, faithful companion

in many adventures and patient helper in the task

of making this book (and her husband)

a little less imperfect.

CONTENTS

ACKNOWLEDGMENTS

I want to give special thanks to many people who have been involved in some way in the birth of this book: students and clients who have given me permission to share their stories; Jen Simmons, for many hours of patiently checking references; Ashley Lare, John Harper, Brig Jones, Ed Marriott, Jay and Carolyn Sklar, Diane Preston, Jack and Lois Easterling, Jennifer Baker and Monty Barker for reading different versions of the manuscript along the way; my colleagues: Robert Vasholz, Nelson Jennings, Michael Williams, Jack Collins, Hans Bayer and David Calhoun for helpful theological, historical and philosophical advice; Drew Blankman, my patient editor at InterVarsity Press; my friend and pastor, Ron Lutjens, who faithfully reminds me of truth and reality; my children, Johanna and John, Matthew and Anna, Rebecca, and Triona, who have encouraged, tolerated and loved a very imperfect father; the board and administration of Covenant Theological Seminary, for the time and encouragement to write; and finally, my dear mother, who has loved faithfully and well, and in her ninety-second year, remains a model of a healthy perfectionist.

INTRODUCTION

Leafing through my files the other day, I found a Father's Day card that my son had given me when he was probably twelve or thirteen. It read, "Dear Dad, They say the sins of the fathers are visited upon the young. In view of the fact that I'm perfect you can't be all that bad yourself." I know only too well that I am not perfect. Yet in some areas of life I would really like to be much better than I am, and I meet many people who struggle to know whether this desire is a good thing or not. It has probably been at least fifteen years since I gave my first lecture on this topic. It was called "Perfectionism: The Road to Heaven or Hell?" This title gives a clue to the pressing dilemma at the heart of this subject: does perfectionism lead people to the heights of achievement and success, or does it cause untold suffering and misery? Perhaps it has potential for both!

Some of the perfectionist tendencies in my own life seem helpful, while some seem more of a hindrance. Each semester, I joke with my students as I give my lecture on perfectionism: "I am writing a book on this subject," I say, "but it is never good enough to be published."

In part, I am entirely serious: each time I prepare that lecture I find myself wanting to clarify a point here and add a few more PowerPoint illustrations there. Using this method, the lecture has, I believe, improved over the years. But when it comes to writing a book, is there a point at which this checking and delaying the final version becomes unhealthy and neurotic?

This morning, with a great sense of relief, after working through the whole manuscript during the last week, I completed a revision of the last chapter. But already, a few hours later, something in me is urging me to go over it yet again. I know I will find things that I do not like, that need to be rewritten. So at times, with typical all-or-nothing thinking, I feel like throwing it out altogether because it will never be good enough. I imagine my family, colleagues or friends reading it and finding endless things to criticize. I feel shame at not having spent more hours perfecting "Perfectionism." But someday soon, I will have to meet my publisher's deadline. And you now know, as you are reading this, I eventually had to accept less than perfection and let the book leave my hands.*

In my own family there is a strong influence of what I consider to be healthy perfectionism, shown in the value that is placed on hard work, high standards, punctuality, cleanliness, tidiness, moral integrity and maintaining good relationships. But what standards are normal? What is healthy? For some of us, perfectionist tendencies verge on the unhealthy, contributing to indecision, procrastination, obsessive behavior, depression and, sometimes, even criticism—almost contempt—for others who do not live up to the same standards. For most of us, a degree of perfectionism has been a good trait that con-

---

*Perhaps a new test for perfectionism could be based on the number of mistakes you find in this book!

tributes to achievement and success and does not damage relationships. But the line is fine and the question recurs: when does trying to be good become bad?

In my years of psychiatric and psychotherapeutic practice I have seen many people who were troubled by different manifestations of perfectionism, from fear of failure and difficulty expressing emotions to severe obsessive-compulsive disorder. I see many men, women and teenagers with all sorts of conflicts about other people's expectations of them—and some troubled by God's expectations, burdened by shame and guilt, feeling that they can never be good enough for him. I have also met highly competent and gifted people for whom perfectionist tendencies were a great asset in their work but a disastrous obstacle in their relationships. Many students, clients and friends have shared their stories and have given permission for me to use them as illustrations.

So I am drawing from a number of different perspectives—personal and family experience, counseling and psychiatry practice, psychological and sociological research, and cultural reflections and theology. In the last fifteen years there has been great interest in perfectionism in the professional literature, and I have spent many hours reading the latest research. I have tried to distill the essence of these studies and to translate the results into nonscientific language without, hopefully, misusing or misinterpreting the conclusions. For anyone who wants more information, I have included references and sometimes notes at the end of the book.

In the first section of the book (chapters 1-3), I introduce the seductive sirens of cultural perfectionism. Having four children—three daughters and a son—I became very aware when they were in their teens of the cultural pressures toward perfection in advertising, in fashion magazines, on TV and in movies. I began to collect examples of advertisements to illustrate my lecture on perfectionism and discovered how frequently the word *perfect* is used in advertising and how often we are offered a quick cosmetic or chemical fix for imperfections in life such as facial wrinkles or anxiety. I have found most of my examples in the United States, but the global movie, music and advertising industries are spreading the same influences around the world, often adjusted and somewhat diluted in other countries. I then delve into definitions of perfectionism and introduce the debate over whether perfectionism is all bad or whether it can be said to have unhealthy and healthy sides. Finally, I describe several different types of perfectionism.

In the second section of the book (chapters 4-6), I focus on the many associations between unhealthy perfectionism and depression, anxiety, procrastination, anorexia nervosa, suicidal tendencies, obsessive-compulsive disorder and other psychological problems.

In the third section of the book (chapters 7-12), I look at genetics, family and cultural influences, shame and pride. In the later part of this section it should become apparent that our worldview and philosophy of life will have a profound influence on what we believe we are intended to be and do.

In the fourth section (chapters 13-15), I discuss practical strategies for change and for learning to live with imperfection. But I cannot end with techniques and strategies as solutions because the problem goes deeper into issues of identity, purpose, human nature and spirituality. To find the foundation of liberation from unhealthy perfectionism, and to discover what it means to pursue excellence and ultimately true perfection, we will explore the heart of Christianity. I hope you will follow me there even if you do not identify yourself as a Christian, as it will help you understand how Christian thought might contribute to healing from unhealthy perfectionism.[†] This section further evaluates the lessons of earlier chapters in a larger theological and philosophical perspective while drawing out the difference such new insights make to day-to-day living. I invite you to join me on this journey of exploration into the world of perfectionism.

[†]For historical reflections on perfectionism in relation to early Greek thought, Christianity and other world religions, see the appendix.

1

THE SEDUCTIVE SIRENS
OF PERFECTIONISM

As I was waiting to board a flight to England, I was searching for a magazine to read, and I noticed a young woman standing alone in front of a whole wall of magazines—*Vogue, Glamour, Shape, Elle, Cosmopolitan*. One magazine cover proclaimed: "The Search for the Perfect Woman." I wondered what it must be like, as a woman, to be faced with such an onslaught of "perfect" models and celebrities with whom to compare one's face, body, clothes and hair. And as I browsed the magazine rack myself, I encountered *Men's Health, GQ, Health and Fitness, Body Builder* and "perfect abs" and huge biceps that made me feel like a wimp! I flipped through the pages of *Gourmet, Town and Country, Better Homes and Gardens, House Beautiful*; each was filled with glossy, beautiful advertisements. The ads highlighted the inadequacies and imperfections of my own life and made me long for a perfect body, a stylish, powerful car and a dream house. I wondered if women, at whom most of the advertisements are directed, would feel similar frustrations with their own lives and, at the same time, deep longings to have a better life and to remain as desirable and beautiful as the "perfect" models portrayed in those magazines.

Many fitness, diet and health magazines promise a wrinkle-free life as well as the latest on how to achieve the perfect weight or fatigue-free existence, how to defy aging and remain young and vibrant— Viagra for your sex life, Botox for facial beauty! Soon, if you do not succumb to the lure of cosmetic surgery, you may begin to feel ugly and old fashioned. In TV shows such as *Extreme Makeover* and *The Swan* women submit to nose jobs, brow lifts, chin augmentation, breast enlargement, liposuction, tummy tucks, skin peels, eye surgery and dental enhancement. They work out with a trainer in the gym and receive fashion advice, hair styling and psychotherapy to help with self-image. All this in the name of "turning the ordinary into the extraordinary," the ugly duckling into the swan! Movies often magnify the tension even more. Everything is larger than life, the colors radiant. Reality seems drab and boring by comparison.

Although I know that most of the photographs of models in magazines are airbrushed and computer-enhanced, something in me does not want to believe it. I want to be like them. And I want to believe that it is possible to be bright and good looking, in a world where brains and beauty are recognized and rewarded. Deep down a voice is telling me not to judge by appearances, but we live in a highly visual age where the vitally important values of character and integrity are very difficult to demonstrate with the same visual impact. Such inner values develop gradually and invisibly. They cannot be technologically accelerated and enhanced in the way that appearance and, to some degree, performance can. Many of our cultural heroes are admired more for their acting or athletic abilities or for their strength and beauty than for their character or ethical integrity.

THE TRIUMPH OF TECHNOLOGY

We have to admit that technology gives us many wonderful things. We can expect instant and flawless communication from just about anywhere in the world. We have exquisite music reproduction in our homes. Cars, at least the ones advertised, are sleek, beautifully crafted pieces of engineering with stunning performance, not to mention the interior complete with a luxury sound system to make even commuting a sensual experience. Lexus, in its "relentless pursuit of perfection," offers the latest model for just $56,000! "The only thing car experts find to criticize," says the advertisement in the *New York Times,* is that it "is so smooth, quiet and perfect . . . it lacks soul."[1]

In every area of life, technology has given us enormous benefits with greater speed, efficiency and remarkable artistic design. In our homes we have innumerable labor-saving devices. Doctors can do amazing things with the latest in laser surgery. Body scanning technology allows us to see into the body without surgical invasion. The secrets of the brain are beginning to be exposed by MRI, CAT and PET scans and other even more sophisticated imaging techniques. Surgical operations can be done by computer from four thousand miles away. Computer-aided special effects have brought us extraordinary scenes in movies such as *The Lord of the Rings, The Matrix* and *Spider-Man.* The pursuit of excellence in technology has certainly been rewarded in remarkable ways.

Designer babies. Technology also promises to overcome our weaknesses and flaws by transforming us into stronger, happier and more intelligent beings. Not only can we get rid of wrinkles and affect brain transmitters with chemicals to get rid of anxiety, depression or aggression, but all sorts of things, both good and bad, become possible with genetic engineering, stem cell research and cloning. Genetic engineering promises to produce "stronger bodies, sharper memories, greater intelligence and happier moods."[2]

Some scientists believe we will be able to enhance the brain with neural implants, improving memory and cognitive ability. Gregory Stock, author of *Redesigning Humans: Our Inevitable Genetic Future*,[3] is an enthusiastic supporter of modifying human beings early in their development. Though critical of Stock's vision of the future, Gina Maranto, author of *Quest for Perfection: The Drive to Breed Better Human Beings*,[4] says, "Individuals will be able to go into a clinic and, through a simple procedure, obtain embryos fitted with chromosomal modules that will slow aging, eliminate disease and enhance personality, temperament, intellect and beauty."[5]

The era of designer babies is upon us. For the moment, in the search for the perfect baby, we use another often positive tool of technology, the ultrasound, to screen for imperfections in babies before birth. Abortion is offered and often advised. "You get questionable news [about a pregnancy] and you make the abortion decision," says Adrienne Asch, a Wellesley bioethicist. "Anything else you do is viewed as stupid by your educated friends, by your doctors, by your genetic counselors." The system, she says, offers too little support for parents who might want to keep an "imperfect" baby.[6] In a future world envisioned in the movie *Gattaca*, embryos are screened for height, sex, IQ and vulnerability to diseases. Already, in our own time, human eggs and sperm are marketed with a high value on intelligence and good looks. In some areas of life this pursuit of perfection has led us to some very difficult ethical and philosophical problems. How much should we tinker with the mind, body and genes to attempt to create the "perfect" person and defy death?

THE PRESSURE FOR PERFECTION

These seductive sirens of the advertising and Hollywood cultures that surround us stimulate our partially conscious fantasies and dreams of perfecting ourselves. They increase our dissatisfaction and discontent with who we are and what we possess. Advances in technology have only enhanced their power and influence. And it is complicated by the fact that the dangerous influences in the pursuit of perfection are, as we have seen, entwined with many good fruits.

Other areas of life are also affected by this dilemma. In the worlds of business, academia and athletics, for example, setting high standards and striving for excellence is greatly valued and highly productive. Miriam Elliott and Susan Meltsner describe the problem in *The Perfectionist Predicament:*

> There's no denying that when you count up material comforts, remarkable achievements, and other outward signs of success, perfectionism will seem to have served you well—especially in this day and age. We have been going through an era in which setting high standards and devoting an inordinate amount of time and energy to attaining them is considered a prerequisite for success. More is better, we are told. Only the best is good enough. It's a jungle out there, and if you're going to survive, you need an edge, an advantage, an ace-in-the-hole. Perfectionism certainly *looks* like it will give you the winning hand and keep you one step ahead of your cutthroat competitors. But appearances can be deceiving.[7]

PROBLEMS WITH PERFECTIONISM

Not only will we find that some aspects of perfectionism prove to be unhealthy and destructive, but when we turn our eyes to other parts of our culture and our world, we see something very different from the affluent, glossy world portrayed by many commercials.

Since the 1960s divorce and crime rates have risen dramatically. Recently the thin veneer of morality in the marketplace has cracked to expose fraud, deception and greed in high places as the optimistic bubble of the stock market popped. The gap between the rich and poor remains enormous in many countries. We have daily reminders of the dark side of human nature in news reports of civil wars and genocide. Despite our great advances in almost every field, it seems as if the human heart has not changed much. The utopian dreams of a peaceful and prosperous earth are far from reality. The achievements of technology raise our hopes and aspirations, stimulate our desires and longings for perfection, but they often leave us frustrated and disappointed as we are constantly reminded that imperfect people do not behave like impersonal and ever-improving machines. The gap between dreams and reality, especially in the area of human relationships and personal fulfillment, does not get any smaller, and our hope of significant advance toward perfection begins to fade.

So we feel the call of the sirens, we know how imperfect we are, and most of us still strive to be better and to improve the quality of our lives. What should we aim for? Is there some objective goal of perfection toward which we *should* strive?

WHAT IS PERFECTION ANYWAY?

We must start our exploration of this subject by looking at how people commonly define perfection and perfectionism. This may open up some questions that will hopefully find their answers later in the book. The word "perfect" derives from the Latin word *perficere*, meaning to make thorough, or complete. *The Oxford English Dictionary* and *Webster's Dictionary* give several related uses of the word: complete in all respects; without defect or omission; flawless; in a condition of complete excellence; faultless; completely correct or accurate; exact; precise.[8]

The *Random House Dictionary* defines *perfection* as

1. The state or quality of being or becoming perfect.

2. The highest degree of proficiency, skill, or excellence, as in some art.

3. A quality, trait, or feature of the highest degree of excellence.[9]

Human beings seem to understand technical perfection most easily. We can measure whether a machine such as a car or a plane is performing with maximum efficiency, but it is a little more difficult to define what maximum efficiency is for a human being unless it is in relation to a skill or proficiency in one area of life, such as performance of a piece of music or a surgical operation.

Another sort of perfection described by philosophers needs a little more explanation. "Teleological" perfection means becoming all that you are supposed to be and finding perfect satisfaction in that state. The Greek word *teleios* is commonly translated "perfect," with the connotation of working toward the *telos,* which means "end." But here we face a question. How are we to know what that "end" is supposed to be? Is that end or purpose defined by scientists, philosophers or theologians? Or is it set by prevailing cultural standards, by parents, by peers or by God?

Throughout history there have been many views on the nature of perfection and whether it is possible to achieve it in this life. In the appendix you will find more detail on the different views of perfectionism throughout history and in each major religion. It was not until the 1930s that the word *perfectionist* was commonly accepted as describing "a person who is only satisfied by the highest standards."[10]

Perfectionism is thus the desire to be unblemished and faultless in some or all areas of life. It is to this contemporary definition of perfectionism that we will turn for a more in-depth study, asking the practical question: is there anything wrong with trying to be the best that we could ever be, in every area of life?

QUESTIONS FOR DISCUSSION

1. How has your view of yourself and of your lifestyle been affected by magazines and advertisements?
2. Do you think that technological advances contribute to the belief that we can perfect ourselves?
3. How do you define perfection?
4. What is a perfect human being?

2

THE PURSUIT OF EXCELLENCE

Healthy or Unhealthy Perfectionism?

In the research literature in the last twenty years there has been a debate about whether all perfectionism is harmful and destructive or whether some forms of it can be helpful and constructive. Some claim that there is a normal, healthy, adaptive form of perfectionism—the pursuit of high standards and excellence—that can be distinguished from neurotic, unhealthy, maladaptive perfectionism. Others claim that attaining perfection is impossible and therefore attempting to reach it is obviously unhealthy. We will look first at the former view.

A SPECTRUM OF PERFECTIONISM

Two leading researchers in this field, Gordon Flett and Paul Hewitt, define perfectionism as "the striving for flawlessness." They write, "Extreme perfectionists are people who want to be perfect in all aspects of their lives."[1] In the simplest terms it is the *tendency* to set extremely high standards, and the use of the word *tendency* implies a spectrum where there are *degrees* of perfectionism. The important issue becomes how strong the *tendency* is, how intensely one strives to reach those standards and how one responds to not meeting them. The size of the discrepancy between what is possible and what is pursued is a critical factor that may make the difference between health and sickness—so also is the intensity with which one attempts to overcome the discrepancy. As the research literature below will repeatedly show, high levels of perfectionism are associated with vulnerability to problems in life, proving that there is a bad side to "being too good."[2]

If we hold this spectrum (also called "multidimensional") view, then neurotic perfectionism is at one end, nonperfectionism is at the other end and somewhere in between is normal, healthy perfectionism, which is characterized by high standards, high levels of organization and striving for excellence.

Neurotic,	Normal,	Non-
Unhealthy – — — — –	Healthy – — — — — — — — –	perfectionism
Perfectionism	Perfectionism	

Normal, healthy perfectionism. Normal, healthy perfectionists are usually full of energy and enthusiasm, have a positive self-image and rarely procrastinate over decisions. They are realistic about their own strengths and weaknesses. They are driven more by a (positive) motivation to achieve than by a (negative) fear of failure. Don Hamachek, a psychologist, writes:

> Normal perfectionists . . . are those who derive a very real sense of pleasure from the labors of a painstaking effort and who feel free to be less precise as the situation permits. . . . Normal perfectionists tend to enhance their self-esteem, rejoice in their skills, and appreciate a job well-done.[3]

Paul is an example of healthy perfectionism. He is a fine surgeon, much respected for his meticulous work in repairing blocked or torn arteries. It is very important that he (and his surgical team) delight in precision. His patients' lives depend on it. A gifted man, he runs a very productive research lab and, in his spare time, plays the violin. He also gives as much time as he can to his family. Somehow he does not need to impose the same meticulous standards on his wife and children that he uses while operating. When he sometimes makes mistakes, he does not endlessly ruminate about how he should have done better.

Many great works of art, music, literature, theology and science have come from such perfectionists. Psychologist Linda Silverman sees perfectionism as a two-edged sword with the potential to propel someone either to unparalleled greatness or into the depths of despair. She writes, "It can best be thought of as an energy that needs to be channeled in positive directions rather than as a malady to be cured."[4]

Neurotic, unhealthy perfectionism. In contrast, neurotic, unhealthy perfectionists set unrealistically high standards. Their sense of self-worth depends entirely on their performance and production according to the goals they set for themselves. Continuous self-criticism, in the form of concern over mistakes and doubts that one is doing the right thing, is a distinguishing mark of unhealthy perfectionism.[5] Hamachek writes again:

> Neurotic perfectionists are the sort of people whose efforts— even their best ones—never seem quite good enough, at least in their own eyes. It always seems to these people that they could—and should—do better. Of course, what this does is to rob them of the satisfaction that might ordinarily accompany a

superior achievement or at least a well-done job . . . because in their own eyes they never seem to do things good enough to warrant that feeling.[6]

For the unhealthy perfectionist, who notices failures more than successes, one flaw obliterates any satisfaction in their achievement. They doubt whether they have done well enough on even the smallest task and judge not just what they do but how they do it. They are often overconcerned about organization, precision and order. They may be fussy and exacting with an emphasis on neatness. "There is a place for everything, and everything must be in its place."[7] They think in all-or-nothing, black-or-white categories. Neurotic perfectionists desire to excel at any cost and are often overcontrolling in relationships. Healthy perfectionists are motivated by a desire to achieve something good whereas unhealthy perfectionists are motivated by fear of negative consequences—failure, rejection or punishment.

Nonperfectionists. At the opposite end of the spectrum from neurotic perfectionists are what we may call nonperfectionists, best defined as those who have little or no shame or guilt about failing to reach high standards or be organized. They are relaxed, easygoing and fun to be around, though perhaps sometimes so laid-back that they are perceived as being disorganized, unreliable and even lazy. Nonperfectionists are very accepting, making few demands on themselves or others—a personality type that can obviously have positive and negative aspects.

The website Despair.com advertises posters that are a good match for nonperfectionists. They sarcastically play off the posters hanging in many corporate offices. One, with the mock-motivational subject *Ineptitude,* shows a skier about to have a terrible fall, and the caption reads, "If you can't learn to do something well, learn to enjoy doing it poorly." Another, under the heading *Mediocrity,* shows the leaning tower of Pisa, and the caption says, "It takes a lot less time and most people won't notice the difference until it's too late."

THE NONSPECTRUM VIEW

The nonspectrum ("unidimensional") view holds that all perfectionism is neurotic and unhealthy and that what I have called "normal" perfectionism should not be labeled perfectionism at all. The qualities of neurotic, unhealthy perfectionism in this view would fall under the label of perfectionism, but the qualities of the normal perfectionist, as described above, would not be called perfectionism at all but would be called conscientiousness, perseverance, an achievement-oriented work style.[8] From this perspective, it is unhelpful and confusing to talk about healthy perfectionism.

Tom Greenspon, author of a helpful book, *Freeing Our Families from Perfectionism,* believes that "healthy perfectionism" is an oxymoron. He writes, "Pursuing excellence, including pushing yourself to do better, constantly improving, setting your goals high, are all fine and are all completely different from perfectionism."[9]

If we agree that all perfectionism is bad, what other words describe what I have called healthy perfectionism? Research has shown that there are five main aspects of personality ("the big five") that seem to remain fairly stable throughout life: neuroticism, extraversion, openness, agreeableness and conscientiousness.[10] The description of conscientiousness seems to parallel our discussion of perfectionism. People who score high on the conscientiousness scale are "competent, orderly, self-disciplined, motivated and careful" in what they do. People who have a low score on this factor are described as "aimless, unreliable, lazy, careless, negligent, weak-willed and hedonistic." This scale contrasts "dependable, fastidious people with those who are lackadaisical and sloppy."[11] High scorers "may become workaholics, low scorers lack ambition."[12] Of course, many people lie somewhere between these extremes. Some say that adaptive, healthy or normal perfectionism should just be called "conscientiousness."[13] Some resort to the phrase "persons of excellence." David Stoop, in pursuing this nonspectrum view has a very helpful chart showing the contrast between perfectionism and persons of excellence.[14] I have added the spectrum view categories in italics.

Perfectionist	Person of Excellence
Unhealthy Perfectionism	*Healthy Perfectionism*
Idealistic	Realistic
Strives for the impossible	Strives for the doable
Fears failure	Anticipates success
Product-minded	Process-minded
Has to be the best	Wants to do their best
Views life as a threat	Views life as a challenge
Hates criticism	Welcomes criticism
Dwells on mistakes	Learns from mistakes
Values self by what they do	Values self for who they are

A WIDER DEBATE

The nonspectrum view pushes toward an all-or-nothing definition of perfectionism in an attempt to avoid ambiguity and uncertainty. Although I have some sympathy for this perspective, I lean more toward what I see as the more practical and commonsense view. Therefore, I will use the spectrum view in the rest of the book, as this seems to be the way language is used in most of the research and in common speech. Most dictionaries acknowledge that, for centuries, the word *perfect* has been modified by such qualifications as more, most, rather, almost and nearly, suggesting degrees of perfection.* I refer to the pursuit of excellence and high standards, to a reasonable degree, as healthy perfectionism, while recognizing a minefield of problems awaiting those who pursue flawless perfection with too much intensity—unhealthy perfectionism.

ACADEMICALLY GIFTED CHILDREN

The difference between healthy and unhealthy perfectionism is illustrated in a fascinating study of sixth grade children. Wayne Parker and Carol Mills studied 820 academically gifted sixth graders (ages 11-12) and found that approximately 33 percent were "nonperfectionist," 42 percent were "healthy perfectionists," and 25 percent were "dysfunctional perfectionists."[15] They described the nonperfec-

> **PERFECTIONISM**
> 25% Dysfunctional perfectionists
> 42% Healthy perfectionists
> 33% Nonperfectionists

tionist group as having low personal standards, low perceived parental expectations, low organization and low total perfectionism scores.†

The healthy perfectionist group had moderately high personal standards, little concern over mistakes, low levels of perceived parental criticism, few doubts about their actions and the highest amount

---

*The *Random House Dictionary* states: "A few usage guides still object to the use of comparison words such as *more, most, nearly, almost* and *rather* with PERFECT on the grounds that PERFECT describes an absolute, yes-or-no condition that cannot logically be said to exist in varying degrees. The English language has never agreed to this limitation. Since its earliest use in the 13th century, PERFECT has, like almost all adjectives, been compared, first in the now obsolete forms PERFECTER and PERFECTEST, or more recently with *more, most,* and similar comparison words: *the most perfect arrangement of color and line imaginable*. PERFECT is compared in most of its general senses in all varieties of speech and writing. After all, one of the objectives of the writers of the U.S. Constitution was 'to form a more perfect union.' "

†These children perceived themselves as being disorganized, unreliable and easily distracted, with a lack of self-discipline. They were also described as having pronounced narcissistic tendencies—presumably only concerned with doing things the way they wanted them and not caring at all about other standards—and broad interests (perhaps making it difficult to focus on one thing for long).

of organization. They were the least neurotic, most agreeable and most conscientious. They were described as organized, dependable, socially skilled, goal- and achievement-oriented, predictable, well adjusted and socially at ease. The strivings of these healthy perfectionists motivated them, in a positive way, to succeed.

The dysfunctional perfectionists (what I have called unhealthy perfectionists) scored in the highest range on the following factors: concern over mistakes, personal standards, parental expectations, perceived parental criticism, doubts about actions and, finally, total scores on a perfectionism scale. They scored highest on neurosis and lowest on agreeableness. They tended to be anxious, socially detached, defensive, moody, and predisposed to be hostile and overly competitive. They also suffered more anxiety and depression.[16] Parker and Mills comment:

> Clearly, striving for excellence can be unhealthy when the striving is unrealistically high. But when dealing with the gifted and talented, it is quite difficult to determine what goals are unrealistic. . . . The distinction between very high levels of achievable expectations and neurotic strivings can be a difficult one to make with talented individuals.[17]

There is some debate about whether perfectionism is more common among gifted students, but the current research suggests that it is not. I suspect that the distribution of perfectionist tendencies in the general population is similar to the distribution among this gifted group of students. Note that an important factor in the unhealthy perfectionists in this study was the perception of parental expectations and criticism. We will return to this theme later.

WHEN HEALTHY BECOMES UNHEALTHY

What is called healthy perfectionism may become unhealthy in some circumstances. I would be delighted to have a window cleaner, painter, architect or brain surgeon who has very high standards and does almost perfect work. Such high standards may be achievable in their work, but to expect the same in relationships with people could be very destructive. When the architect goes home at night, he should not expect such meticulous attention to detail and order from his wife and children.

Becky was a wonderful high school teacher. Her students greatly respected her, and she helped many of them to achieve high standards and entrance to the best colleges and universities. But when she had her first baby—who was, like most newborns, rather unpredictable and messy, with no regular sleep rhythm—she felt she was losing control. She began to see herself as a failure as a mother, and she spiraled down into serious depression. The high expectations she had in one area of life were inappropriate for a newborn baby.

Driving or defeated perfectionism. I would love to always be able to keep my desk neat and tidy—a place for everything and everything in its place! There are times when I work hard to keep it that way and other times when I give up in the face of piles of unanswered mail, papers to be filed, and other bits and pieces that seem to accumulate there. Then I think, *Why bother to even try?*

TWO SIDES OF PERFECTIONISM

adaptive, positive, healthy, constructive

- high standards
- good self-esteem
- strive for excellence
- realistic about failures
- organized
- energy and enthusiasm

maladaptive, negative, unhealthy, destructive

- unrealistically high standards
- low self-esteem
- seek to excel at any cost
- generalize failure
- controlling
- exhausted and exhausting

People sometimes say, "Oh, I am not a perfectionist. Look at my clothes that need ironing, my chaotic room, my poor grades." But is it possible to be a defeated perfectionist, inwardly wanting everything so perfect that anything less is not worth aiming for so that we don't bother to try at all or we give up trying?

Some people are active and energetic in their pursuit of excellence. They push themselves—and sometimes others—hard and are usually very productive in what they achieve. But they may drive themselves too hard, often because their identity and self-worth depend on succeeding at everything. One failure for such a driven person might be enough to tip the scales from a healthy pursuit of excellence to self-destructive perfectionism. Paralysis may ensue with fear of mistakes, self-doubt, indecision and procrastination to the point of passivity and utter defeat. Below is a story of a man who seems to have crossed the line from driving to defeated perfectionism.

Vince Foster was a gifted lawyer and deputy counsel to the president who, at the peak of his career, took his own life. Foster graduated first in his law school class and scored highest on the Arkansas bar exam. In his work, he "researched each case extensively . . . and would go through 20 drafts if he had to. He could be demanding."[18] "According to one professional associate, Foster seemed to have known only success: 'I never saw a professional setback. . . . He seemed to glide through life.' He was intensely hard working and fiercely loyal."[19] A few months before his death, Foster delivered the commencement address at the University of Arkansas Law School. He emphasized the importance of one's reputation:

> The reputation you develop for intellectual and ethical integrity will be your greatest asset or your worst enemy. . . . There is no victory, no advantage, no fee, no favor which is worth even a

blemish on your reputation for intellect and integrity. . . . Dents to the reputation in the legal profession are irreparable.[20]

As the note written shortly before his death indicated, Foster was deeply upset by the editorials in the *Wall Street Journal* concerning his role in the Clinton administration, editorials questioning his integrity both in Washington and back home in Little Rock in the Rose Law Firm. He believed that they "had tarnished his reputation."[21] Believing he was disgraced in Washington and perceived as a failure in Little Rock, Foster probably felt he had nowhere to go. This "tower of strength" took his own life in July 1993.[22]

Apart from conspiracy theories that float around his death, there is some evidence that he was suffering from clinical depression for some weeks before this final, desperate act. Foster's failure to live up to his own incredibly high standards of perfection cost him dearly. He swung from the feeling of being a great success to being a terrible failure.

Defeated perfectionists often become victims of their own high standards. They carry in their heads, partially subconscious, a picture of who they want to be and who they firmly believe they can and should be: their ideal self. When things are going well, they almost live up to this fantasy, but as soon as something goes wrong, as soon as some flaw or failure is noticeable, then their tendency to all-or-nothing thinking takes hold. They often perceive themselves as complete disasters: despicable, unreliable, incompetent people. Their ideal self and their perceived self are polar opposites. The inner tension is unbearable. The truth, which is rarely visible to them, is that their real self is somewhere in between the two. But it is almost impossible, without help, time and patience, for such a person to hold the two poles in a creative tension and live in the real world of both success *and* failure. It is this perceived discrepancy between "who I think I should be" and "who I think I really am" that is at the heart of the pain of perfectionism.[23] The driven perfectionist works harder to close the gap; the defeated perfectionist gives up the fight.[24] The healthy perfectionist is able to live in the tension.

CONCLUSION

You can see that the problem with perfectionism begins when we move beyond the legitimate pursuit of excellence to live under the tyranny of believing that perfection is possible and failures are unacceptable. Standards of productivity, accomplishment or appearance are so high that they are impossible to attain. When our self-worth and self-respect depend on reaching those standards, the result is an inevitable script for self-defeat: one's own personal hell of repeated failure, self-criticism and depression.

Notice that it is the degree of intensity with which we pursue impossible goals, and the degree to which we feel that our worth is dependent on reaching those goals, that defines the difference between healthy and unhealthy perfectionism. In the next chapter we will look at different types of perfectionism—because each person experiences and expresses it in different ways.

QUESTIONS FOR DISCUSSION

1. Before you read this chapter, did you think of perfectionism as all bad or as partially bad and partially good?

2. What traits of (a) healthy and (b) unhealthy perfectionism do you see in yourself and your family?

3. In what areas of life do you think you are a perfectionist?

4. What is the difference between your "ideal self" and your "perceived self"?

3

TYPES OF PERFECTIONISM

Some people are perfectionists in only one or two areas of life. Miriam Elliott and Susan Meltsner in *The Perfectionist Predicament: How to Stop Driving Yourself and Others Crazy* give a helpful and popular classification: performance, appearance, interpersonal, moral and all-around perfectionists.[1]

A POPULAR CLASSIFICATION SYSTEM

Performance perfectionist. Performance perfectionists' sense of value is highly dependent on how they perform, whether as athletes, musicians, writers or in some other field of expertise. Measurable productivity and achievement is vital to their sense of well-being. Their life motto is "I achieve, therefore I am." If they are unable to produce or perform at peak levels they usually become depressed and anxious. They aim for good colleges and good jobs and usually achieve their goals but pay a price in anxiety and worry.

One young woman, who was beginning to realize how her perfectionism was not always helpful, said:

Throughout my childhood I craved my family's and friends' approval so I strove to excel in any area that would allow achievement to be attained. I was an A student. . . . I excelled in sports and participated in school plays and select choirs. I even cheated on an exam in ninth grade to excel at any cost. By my junior year in high school I was burned out and exhausted. . . . The times I did fail were devastating. Any grade below A was not acceptable. In playing basketball and tennis any shot missed proved to me I was a failure and drove me to practice more and work harder.

There are examples from many walks of life. You might think that salespeople who are conscientious, hardworking perfectionists would sell more than their less conscientious competitors, but those who score high on a perfectionism scale actually sell less than those who have mid-range scores.[2] Athletes who are perfectionists have a much harder time recovering from failure and therefore may not perform as well overall.[3] Most elite athletes feel driven to aim for a "perfect" performance. Setting high standards is essential to their sport. But athletes who are overconcerned about making mistakes tend to have greater difficulty concentrating, more negative thinking and less self-confidence before they compete.[4]

Appearance perfectionist. Appearance perfectionists are most concerned about how they look. Their motto is "I am how I look!" A woman may spend much time and money on makeup, hair, clothes and weight loss regimes to ensure a flawless appearance. Similarly, men may spend hours at the gym and in front of a mirror building and toning their bodies. Their standard will probably be heavily influenced by the images in fashion and fitness magazines. Impression management dominates their lives.

One of my students told me of the increasing pressure she felt as a teenager to be "perfect." Throughout high school she spent hours watching MTV and teen television shows, being bombarded with images of female seduction and beauty. She constantly compared herself to these people and began working to emulate them. She told me:

No matter how hard I worked at putting on makeup, wearing the "right" clothes, buying the top 10 CDs, I never felt good enough. I never left the house feeling confident about my looks or my body or my clothes, and I certainly felt terrible if I was seen in jeans and a T-shirt. I felt actual shame for not looking like my favorite actresses, singers and models.

Preoccupation with appearance may extend to home, garden, car and children. It is fine to have a neat, orderly and good-looking home, but desire for perfection can become an all-consuming passion. A friend, whose perfectionism was partially channeled constructively into making finely embroidered children's dresses, would not allow her children to have friends stay at their house lest they leave dirty finger marks on the walls. Anticipation of visitors would make her so anxious that she would clean and tidy until the house looked immaculate and then cover the carpets with newspaper!

Interpersonal perfectionism. Interpersonal perfectionists have very set ideas about the way things should be done, and this tends to make relationships difficult. With an outward focus, they may be very critical and demanding of others and therefore become isolated. With an inward focus, they may be very self-critical and therefore avoid relationships for fear of being discovered for who they really are: flawed and imperfect! Greg was an attractive and charming forty-year-old stock broker who came to see me because he desperately wanted to get married. As his story unfolded, I discovered that whenever his girlfriends started to get too close and intimate, wanting to know more about his thoughts, feelings and inner world, Greg would get scared that his flaws would be discovered and would begin to retreat. His fear would express itself with increasingly critical comments about little things that his girlfriend did or said until, inevitably, the relationship ended. His perfectionism about himself was hidden behind his perfectionistic expectations of others.

Moral perfectionism. Moral perfectionists are concerned that they and all those around them should keep the rules or laws exactly and meticulously, and they will go out of their way to make sure this happens. Their motto might be "I behave perfectly therefore I am." One client told me of a relative who would always drive at five miles per hour below the speed limit lest he break the law. The classic biblical example of moral perfectionism is the attitude of the Pharisees of Jesus' time. They created and enforced hundreds of extra rules and regulations. There was a general law that people should not work on the sabbath, but the Pharisees created thirty-nine categories of actions that were forbidden on that day. They were outraged when Jesus healed a man on the sabbath. This type of perfectionism might also manifest itself in personal rules of etiquette and behavior that the moral perfectionist thinks are self-evident and should be followed by everyone else. This is often called *legalism.*

All-around perfectionism. All-around perfectionists are concerned with high standards and excellence in every area of life. Performance, appearance and morality are all extremely important. The all-around perfectionist merges into what we call the obsessive personality where there is great concern about order, organization, rules and lists, and great attention to detail. Their motto might be "I am perfectly in control, therefore I am."

James was a computer analyst. Each day he would arrive at his office exactly ten minutes before 8:00. He was meticulously careful not to extend his lunch hour and would always stay a few minutes after 5:00. Some days he would stay long into the evening to finish a job, checking and rechecking that he had done it properly. Each week, he color-coded every minute of the day in his day planner, and he would become very anxious if he was asked to do tasks that forced him to deviate from his regular routine. Although his colleagues admired his efficiency and moral integrity, they were often frustrated by his lack of flexibility. He was a responsible husband and father but expected almost perfect behavior and grades from his children. At times he could be humorous and lighthearted with his wife, but most of the time she felt he was trying too hard to be a "good" husband. Their sexual relationship was governed by his need to be in control; it therefore became routine and so boring for his wife that she lost interest. Such rigidity in most areas of life is characteristic of the all-around perfectionist and the obsessive personality.

I have described a popular classification of types of perfectionism. Here is another system that has emerged from the research on perfectionism.

AN ACADEMIC CLASSIFICATION SYSTEM

The Multidimensional Perfectionism Scale was developed by Paul Hewitt and Gordon Flett in 1991; it is based not so much on the area of life involved but on the focus and direction of the perfectionism. They describe three types of perfectionism, with the rather awkward and less immediately understood names of self-oriented, socially prescribed and other-oriented perfectionism.[5] My description of the characteristics of these types and their assets and liabilities is drawn directly from the research literature, which relies largely on the use of these terms, and may at times feel stilted. Remember that very few people are purely one type or another, but one type may be particularly dominant.

Self-oriented perfectionism. Self-oriented perfectionists (SOPs) set high and often rigid standards for themselves. They work hard to attain perfection and avoid failure. They are self-critical and tend to focus on their flaws and failings. They take responsibility for their lives and do not blame others when they fail.

These people, often very successful, are usually described by others in very positive ways. SOPs are usually self-confident, charming and quietly assertive. They are conscientious, organized and disciplined. In relationships they are usually agreeable, thoughtful and empathic. They often have strong moral standards and well-developed consciences.

There is much here that is adaptive and healthy, very often including a confidence in coping with stress and handling difficult situations. However, as the strength of their perfectionism increases and moves into the unhealthy and neurotic range, problems begin to emerge in relationships. Feeling inferior and unworthy of friendship and fearing rejection when another

SELF-ORIENTED PERFECTIONISM

Normal/Healthy
- self-assured
- assertive
- conscientious
- organized
- disciplined
- determined
- diligent
- thoughtful
- courteous
- empathic
- helpful
- strong moral standards
- sensitive conscience

Neurotic/Unhealthy
- depressed
- impatient
- self-blaming
- shame and guilt
- irritable
- angry
- fears criticism
- avoids challenges
- suicidal tendencies

person really gets to know them, SOPs will tend to keep their distance from other people. They will be friendly on the surface, anxious to please, though often not very self-revealing. In addition, they may be so concerned with making a good impression and organizing life with lists of things to *do,* that they find it difficult to just *be* in a relationship. To others, they sometimes appear irritable, impatient and competitive.[6] Fearing rejection, they often react defensively to criticism. This frustrates others and often produces the disapproval they fear, thus reinforcing the conviction that they have to be perfect to be accepted.

At high levels and especially under certain types of stress, this type of perfectionism can be destructive. The normally adaptive coping mechanisms are overwhelmed, leading to depression, fear of criticism, shame, guilt and, sometimes, as we have seen in the case of Vince Foster, suicidal tendencies.

Socially prescribed perfectionism. Socially prescribed perfectionists (SPPs) are driven not so much by their own high standards but by the belief that other significant people (parents, peers, professors, God) hold very high standards for them, which, in order to be accepted, they must strive to achieve at all costs. It is obviously normal and healthy to feel some family and social expectation to do well. The SPP, however, is haunted to an abnormal degree by what they think other people's expectations are of them, and they greatly fear rejection. In contrast to self-oriented perfectionism, where, at low levels, there are many positive and healthy traits, the research finds very little that is positive about socially prescribed perfectionism.

SPPs feel that they are being rigorously evaluated by others. They believe that every flaw and failure will be noticed, so they have to work hard to achieve what they imagine is the other person's standard. They struggle with fear of making mistakes and doubts about whether their actions are right. They may be silently angry that they have to live this way, resenting others for demanding it of them. At the same time, they blame themselves for not being good enough.

Since they do not believe that they have the ability to live up to others' expectations, they may eventually feel helpless and hopeless, often avoiding relationships and risks in potentially stressful and challenging situations. For such people, their worlds are filled with people who are dissatisfied with them and critical of their performance. The unhealthy perfectionist is in a bind, desiring relationships but finding them to be unreliable and full of conflict.[7]

SOME PERILS OF PERFECTIONISM

- excessive checking and seeking reassurance
- anxiety and worry
- decreased productivity and performance
- impaired health
- eating disorders
- depression
- suicidal ideas
- obsessive-compulsive symptoms
- scrupulosity
- relationship problems

This type of perfectionism is associated with many problems, such as test anxiety and procrastination, loneliness, discouragement, sadness, depression, anxiety, eating disorders and psychosomatic disorders. They do not cope well with stress, and their reactions to stress only exacerbate the difficulties of the situation.

Other-oriented perfectionism. Other-oriented perfectionists (OOPs) often appear confident, self-assured and capable, yet they are concerned not so much with achieving certain standards for themselves but with demanding perfection from those around them. They tend to be self-centered and rather insensitive to the needs of others. We have met them before in what I called the outward-focused (interpersonal) perfectionist. Long-term relationships are difficult because these individuals tend to be controlling, competitive, self-centered, impatient and arrogant. You might be able to tolerate them as a basketball coach for a single season but not as a spouse or long-term friend!

Again, it is reasonable to have some expectations of others. I legitimately expect the pilot of the plane in which I am flying to be meticulous. I expect my car mechanic to be well trained and to do a good job, especially as I am paying him enough for the safety of a well-functioning car. I expect my students to study hard and get good grades. But to expect perfection and flawless performances from everyone, whether pilot, mechanic, secretary, colleague, student, father, mother, wife or child, will alienate me from reality and from all deep relationships.

James came to see me because he was lonely and longing to be married. He was charming and successful, but he left a trail of brokenhearted women behind him. No one was quite good enough. For James, there was always something not quite right about the women that he dated. As I listened to his sad story, I kept hearing the words I first heard from Edith Schaeffer in my head, "If you demand perfection, you will end up with nothing!"

> **OTHER-ORIENTED PERFECTIONISTS**
>
> *May be confident and successful but often have difficult relationships with tendencies to be*
> - domineering
> - controlling
> - competitive
> - self-centered
> - disagreeable
> - blaming
> - impatient
> - distant
> - arrogant

Unhealthy levels of perfectionism. Numerous studies have been done which demonstrate that socially prescribed perfectionism is associated with far more problems than self-oriented or other-oriented perfectionism. OOP is associated with some problems, while SOP seems to be the least problematic, especially at lower levels of intensity, and is in fact associated with many positive attributes. However, SOP, while normally healthy and productive, can become negative when the person is under pressure from cumulative, stressful life events. It is as if there is, for each person, a critical point of pressure and stress at which previously adaptive qualities become maladaptive.

In general, perfectionists tend to have difficulties with any new and unpredictable situation. The known, familiar and repeated are comfortable and secure. The perfectionist is able to maintain an appearance of being relaxed and in control, but under that thin veneer there are many frightening emotions that must be controlled at all costs.

A study of medical, dental, nursing and pharmacy students found that over one-quarter of the students were experiencing "psychiatric levels of distress." Obviously students in these particular fields are high achievers, and some degree of perfectionism is an asset. But those who were more strongly perfectionist, especially those who were worried about meeting others' expectations, reported a greater number of psychological symptoms.[8]

Another study considered 104 female executives ranging in age from thirty-six to fifty-two. Those who were strong perfectionists experienced more problems with stress, burnout, depression, low self-esteem and symptoms of physical illness.[9] Because of their unrealistically high standards, excessive concerns about making mistakes and doubts about their performance, any "increase in daily hassles" was seen as a threat to their ability to cope. Humor and optimism were low in the highly perfectionist women but seemed to have a positive role in dealing with stress for the other women. The highly perfectionist women tended to cope by trying hard to deal with stresses independently and by blaming themselves when things went wrong. In contrast, those who were less perfectionist delegated responsibility, sought emotional support from others and were more self-accepting in challenging situations. Highly perfectionist women tended to see difficulties as personally threatening and dangerous, whereas the other women were able to see the difficulties as a challenging learning experience. These studies help to illustrate that high levels of self-oriented perfectionism tend to be generally negative, but moderate levels have quite positive effects.

Jack, a student of mine, described the difficult relationship he had with his perfectionist parents, especially his father. Jack's story illustrates some of the positive and negative aspects of the different types of perfectionism. His father grew up on a small farm and was valedictorian in his high school graduating class, but he could not afford to go to college. He worked hard and by the time he was thirty, he started his own business and was operating a Burger King franchise. Jack told me, "We were not a close family; we were a driven family. Expectations were high, and if they were not met, there were consequences."

Jack's mother kept a spotless house. She was constantly cleaning and organizing, and her life was very regimented and predictable. Meals were strictly programmed so that the family ate the same food on the same day each week: macaroni and cheese, cured ham and green beans every Monday night; pork chops, green peas and dumplings on Tuesdays . . .

His father was, and still is, a very dominant figure in the family.* He was a workaholic, often working seventy hours a week even when he did not need to, so his children did not see him much. When he did come home, things were not pleasant.

---

*Jack's father is a performance perfectionist with a combination of self-oriented, socially prescribed and strong other-oriented traits. Jack's mother is an appearance, performance and self-oriented perfectionist. Jack is a socially prescribed performance perfectionist.

He expected only the best; we had to make straight As, we had to be the best-behaved, well-mannered children, and we had to be the best tennis players (even though he never watched any of us play because he was at work). . . . As expected, I, like my brothers, often failed to live up to his expectations. The result was discipline, as well as criticism for not achieving only the best. Dad was a very hard disciplinarian; however, while he did not spare the rod, he was not physically abusive. Love was seldom expressed, either verbally or by body language.

Jack went to work when he was fourteen and, after graduating from college, married and went to work for his dad, just as his older brother had before him. He started out as an assistant manager, gradually working his way up to director of operations. This promotion put him in close physical proximity to his father, something that hadn't happened since he moved out of the house ten years earlier. The job that he loved for six years now changed drastically because he was once again "under Dad's microscope." Eager to meet his father's impossible standards and expectations, Jack, himself, became a workaholic and ignored his family. The company excelled over the next ten years, expanding and winning many national awards, but Jack's relationship with his father slowly declined because, he told me, "I couldn't live up to his expectations; it didn't matter how many hours I worked."

Jack and his wife decided to leave the business because it was negatively affecting their own family and because the relationship with his parents was collapsing. He continued:

There were lots of wounds—constant criticism of how my wife cleaned the house, things I needed to improve on at work, how we raised our kids (even how we fed our kids), the friends we had and where we went to church. Dad wanted input and control over everything we were involved in. . . . Never measuring up to Dad's standards has certainly impacted my confidence in doing almost anything—I seldom feel that I am capable.

SIX KEY FEATURES AND FOUR IMPORTANT FACTORS OF PERFECTIONISM

Earlier in this chapter I introduced you first to a popular classification system and then to the Multidimensional Perfectionism Scale developed by Hewitt and Flett. The latter described perfectionism in terms of relational styles: self-oriented, socially prescribed and other-oriented. Rather confusingly, another scale with the same name was developed at approximately the same time by Randy Frost and his team. This scale did not classify *relationship styles* or *types* of perfectionism but developed a scale that defined and measured six *key features* of the inner thought life of perfectionists.

The Frost MPS (Multidimensional Perfectionism Scale) found the following six factors to be central to perfectionism: (1) Excessive concern over mistakes in performance. This they describe as the "major dimension." (2) Excessively high personal standards of performance. (3) Doubting the quality of one's performance. (4) Perception of high parental expectations. (5) Perception of high parental criticism. (6) An exaggerated emphasis on precision, order and organization.[10] These themes have recurred throughout this chapter's exploration.

Yet another group, Robert Slaney and his colleagues, has developed the Almost Perfect Scale (APS-Revised) in which they describe four factors at the heart of perfectionism: high standards, orderliness, tendencies to procrastinate and problems with relationships. They differentiate between adaptive and maladaptive perfectionism. High standards and orderliness are strongly associated with adaptive (healthy) perfectionism. "Discrepancy," the perception that one consistently fails to meet the high standards one has set for oneself, is associated with maladaptive (unhealthy) perfectionism.[11]

CONCLUSION

In this chapter we have seen something of the nature of perfectionism. I have described the different ways of classifying it and given you a taste of some of the research of the last fifteen years, hopefully demonstrating that perfectionism, as we have defined it, has both healthy and unhealthy aspects. In the next few chapters, we will look, in greater detail, at the price that is paid by those who struggle with unhealthy perfectionism.

QUESTIONS FOR DISCUSSION

1. If there are perfectionist tendencies in you and your family, how do you and they fit into the two classification systems (popular and academic) described in this chapter?

2. Do you tend to set very high standards for yourself and think that you consistently fail to reach them?

3. Do the differences between the three academic types of perfectionism ring true in your experience?

4. In what ways have you seen perfectionism help or hinder relationships?

4

DEPRESSION, ANGER AND EATING DISORDERS

In this section we will look at some research on the serious problems associated with perfectionism. We will start with depression and end with anorexia nervosa, both problems in which self-criticism is a prominent ingredient. In between we will touch on anger.

DEPRESSION

While a healthy degree of perfectionism may reduce the risk of depression, higher levels of perfectionism can *lead* to depression. Healthy perfectionism, characterized by hard work, high standards, conscientiousness and organization, leads to a sense of achievement, well-being and hope that the future can at least be partially controlled,[1] thus protecting against depression. These are the individuals "for whom perfectionist strivings motivate rather than paralyze; for whom perfectionism spurs rather than inhibits achievement."[2] By contrast, unhealthy perfectionists who measure high on three

scales—concern over mistakes, doubts about actions and hopelessness about the future—are more likely to be depressed and to enter-
tain suicidal ideas.

All perfectionists tend to be very goal oriented and become easily
discouraged if their goals are frustrated or blocked. They also tend to
be very self-critical when under pressure.[3] Such individuals experience a failure or stressful life event, such as being fired from a job or
getting a speeding ticket, as a failure of control.[4] For all of us, of
course, it is the interpretation of events, rather than the events themselves, that determines how stressful they are. So, says researcher
Paul Hewitt, it is the perfectionist's tendency to "stringently evaluate,
focus on negative aspects of performance, and experience little satisfaction"[5] that increases the risk of depression.

Burnout. Another result of perfectionism, which is closely related
to depression, is burnout. One pastor, who was prone to perfectionism, told me about his shame as he experienced loss of enthusiasm
for his work, increased cynicism about people, a sense of hopelessness and failure, difficulty making decisions, and a lack of energy—
classical symptoms of burnout and depression. He believed that
there was considerable conflict between the congregation and himself about his role in the church. He was tempted to measure success
by the size of the congregation. Yet because his congregation was a
small one, he always felt like a failure. Due to his fear of not being or
doing the best, he tended to be indecisive and to avoid conflict. He
had grown up in a family of high achievers and felt that, by comparison, his own achievements had been unspectacular and modest, far
from "good enough." This perfectionism made him more vulnerable
to emotional exhaustion as the pressures built up around him in the
church. As a result, he became increasingly paralyzed.

Suicidal ideation. Many brilliant people have been tormented by perfectionist tendencies. Ludwig Wittgenstein, the German philosopher, was a nervous and obsessive individual who struggled throughout his life with depressive moods and suicidal thoughts and urges. His extremely negative thoughts seem to have arisen from his frustration at and guilt over not being perfect. He had apparently absorbed from his father a powerful sense of duty, often feeling guilty over relatively trivial matters and displaying the highest ideals for himself.[6] The writer Sylvia Plath held herself and others to very high standards. Unable to keep them she eventually gave in to her suicidal tendencies, taking her own life in 1962, in the middle of a brilliant career. [7]

Earlier we looked at the last days of Vince Foster, the perfectionist White House lawyer, as he slipped into a depression that ended in suicide. The story of Admiral Boorda is a similar case. In 1996 Boorda, much to everyone's surprise, took his own life. Because he had risen through the ranks to be the Navy's senior admiral, Boorda was much appreciated by the lower ranks and well respected by everyone. Despite this widespread popularity, he found it hard to believe this. Boorda was described as an excellent officer who was sensitive but driven. Although he did not need to enhance his reputation, it was perhaps a deep sense of inferiority that drove him to overcompensate by adding two bronze, combat Vs (for valor), which he had not earned, to two of his ribbons. When his foolish self-inflation was exposed, his shame at being publicly humiliated drove him to another extreme reaction. Shortly before a press conference, during which he would have had to answer questions about what he had done, Boorda took his own life.[8]

Perfectionist individuals, with their high standards and concern about making mistakes, may experience intense shame when faced with even a small failure. With all-or-nothing thinking, they may swing from great confidence to extreme hopelessness. Perfectionist adolescents, whose natural tendency toward idealism is twice as strong as their peers', are particularly at risk of intense mood swings. Suicidal attempts are often precipitated by shameful events such as a failure at school or work, an arrest, or a conflict with, or perceived rejection by, a lover or parent.[9]

After discussing the suicides of several prominent people, psychiatrist Sidney Blatt summarizes the problem well as he concludes:

> These accounts . . . are typical of numerous examples of talented, ambitious, and successful individuals who are driven by intense needs for perfection and plagued by intense self-scrutiny, self-doubt, and self-criticism. Powerful needs to succeed and to avoid possible public criticism and the appearance of defect force some individuals to work incessantly hard to achieve and accomplish but always leave them profoundly vulnerable to the criticism of others and to their own self-scrutiny and judgment. This harsh punitive superego can be a driving force for achievement, but it can also result in little satisfaction in accomplishments, and through a marked vulnerability to experiences of failure and criticism, in an increased susceptibility to ensuing depression and suicide. Because of the need to maintain a personal and public image of strength and perfection, such individuals are constantly trying to prove themselves, are always on trial, feel vulnerable to any possible implication of failure or criticism, and often are unable to turn to others, even to the closest of confidants, for help or to share their anguish.[10]

ANGER

For the perfectionist whose expectations are unattainable and inflexible, there is usually intense frustration when something does not work out quite right, a mistake is made, a goal is not met, or people and circumstances are not predictable and controllable. Other-oriented perfectionists will express their anger with the people around them, whereas the self-oriented and socially prescribed perfectionists will berate themselves for their incompetence and then for their loss of control in showing their emotions. Because perfectionists are fearful of losing control and are so anxious to please others, they will often hold anger inside, and it may surface in minor irritation, moodiness, depression, anxiety or, if provoked enough, sudden explosions of rage.

EATING DISORDERS

We now turn to disorders that are much more common in young women, although 10 percent of people who struggle with them are male. There is a strong connection between perfectionism and eating disorders. Healthy perfectionism—where there is an enjoyment of high standards, a need for order and organization, and a healthy acceptance of and care for one's body—does not increase vulnerability to eating disorders, but unhealthy perfectionism significantly increases the risk, especially if there is strong concern about making mistakes and doubt about one's actions.[11] Women suffering with anorexia often feel that they are failing in other areas in life, so they find comfort and achievement in mastering their weight.

Psychotherapist Hilde Bruch described her young anorexic patients as being excessively compliant, approval seeking and studious. She believed that they had deep needs for control and perfection arising from pervasive feelings of ineffectiveness and inadequacy.[12] Her patients compensated, she believed, for a fearful, empty, real self by living behind the mask of a false self who was confident, capable and always did the right thing. Women with eating disorders have a strong need to appear perfect and to avoid disclosing any imperfection. They are extremely sensitive to others' opinions and have an intense desire for approval.[13] Since they can control their weight, this becomes their source of worth and identity. It gives a sense of "mastery, virtue and self-control"[14] in one area of life when everything else feels perilously out of control.[15]

Pauline's story illustrates the typical themes of anorexia. She was reluctant to see a doctor or counselor, but her parents brought her to see me because they were very worried about her weight loss and her preoccupation with food and exercise. One of her mother's friends had had a daughter who died of anorexia nervosa just one year before. Her father was a very successful lawyer who drove himself very hard and loved his work. Her mother did not work outside home, but she enjoyed cooking for her family and was very slim.

At school, Pauline was a good student and excelled in swimming, gymnastics and tennis. During that same year she entered a beauty contest and came in second. She believed that she would have won if her thighs and buttocks had been smaller, so she started dieting. This resulted in arguments with her mother, who thought that she was already too thin. Pauline's solution was to offer to do the cooking so that she could keep control of her calorie intake. During meals she moved the food around on the plate so that she appeared to be eating. She spent long hours in her room "studying" and in the evenings attended gymnastics classes. In her room she exercised strenuously for 15-20 minutes every two hours and played music to hide the noise of her exercise from her parents. She told them that the music helped her to concentrate on her studies. She became obsessive about her weight, weighing herself before and after eating, exercising and going to the bathroom.

She was chosen to represent her state in a gymnastics competition, so she increased her daily exercise. Her weight dropped from 115 to 96 pounds, but she wore loose clothes to disguise her figure. One day, when her mother was helping her to buy a dress, she saw her daughter almost naked and was horrified at her emaciated appearance, so they began to seek help. In therapy, Pauline confessed that, in addition to not feeling pretty enough or good enough, some of her anorexia was a form of self-punishment because she felt guilty about a time when she had been drunk and too intimate with a boyfriend.

The themes in this story are common to many families with an anorexic teen—high achieving, somewhat anxious parents, an anorexic's own shame and guilt, failure in competition, a broken relationship, dieting, exercise and deceit. Perfectionist patterns—all-or-nothing thinking, fear of rejection and the desire to be in control—are clear.

Another client, Megan, struggled on the edge of anorexia all through high school, envious of other girls who had "perfect" bodies.* In college, hundreds of miles from home, she was overwhelmed by loneliness and used overeating to comfort herself and to numb her feelings. Once a binge began she would not stop until her stomach was swollen, and then she would resort to secrecy and subterfuge to find a dorm bathroom where she could be alone to get rid of the food—until the next time. She was in the grip of anorexia and bulimia.

When emotional pain is dulled in this way and the achievement of the perfect weight and shape gives such a powerful sense of identity, it is not surprising that it is hard to acknowledge that there is any-

---

*Eating disordered women are sensitive to the need to conform to the ideal of beauty portrayed by models, Hollywood stars and their peers; they become easy victims of the seductions of fashion magazines and health and beauty trends. In a later chapter we will see how powerful the media images are in shaping young people's view of how they should look.

thing wrong with this behavior. To the anorexic, self-control feels so right and good. Furthermore, people with eating disorders often "list themes of purity, cleanliness, godliness and stoicism as important values."[16] Strangely, the starving, bingeing and purging help to get rid of the feelings of shame and guilt—for a while anyway. These actions may even be justified by the person with anorexia or bulimia as a higher form of spirituality that involves self-denial, fasting and prayer.

From a consideration of depression, suicidal thoughts and eating disorders, we turn in the next chapter to problems of excess anxiety associated with perfectionism.

QUESTIONS FOR DISCUSSION

1. Why does perfectionism make people vulnerable to depression?

2. Think of examples in your own life or in the lives of those around you where you see the connection between perfectionist thought patterns and depressive moods or severe depression.

3. Control of weight is obviously a central aspect of anorexia. Discuss the relationship of desire for control and perfectionism.

4. How is emotional pain "dulled" by starving, bingeing or purging?

5

WORRY, ANXIETY AND OBSESSIONS

Susannah spent many hours working on the chemistry paper, even doing an all-nighter as the deadline drew near. When she got a B, she was devastated, feeling as if she was a complete failure—a disappointment to her teacher and her parents. David came second in a high school track event and felt that he had let down his team. He was afraid that his teammates would not like him after his "failure," despite the fact that several of them had not come in first in their events either.

Most people worry to some degree, but worry about making mistakes, about making the wrong decision, about what others think, about doing well enough, and about failure and rejection are all a daily part of the negative side of a perfectionist's life. Beneath these fears is a deep desire to gain approval and acceptance and to avoid shame and humiliation.[1]

Pefectionism is also associated with performance anxiety, procrastination, indecisiveness and obsessive-compulsive disorder

(OCD), each of which we will explore in more detail.

PERFORMANCE ANXIETY

For artists, performers and athletes, some anxiety can give a helpful shot of adrenaline that stimulates a fine performance, but higher levels of anxiety can be paralyzing. Significant perfectionism is associated more with performance paralysis than with facilitating anxiety. The former may be expressed in the form of worry and fear or in physical symptoms of anxiety such as trembling, sweating, rapid heartbeat, chest pain, hyperventilation and feeling faint.

Athletes who are very concerned about making mistakes report mental images of failure, difficulty concentrating and worry about the response of the audience. They tend to ruminate about the threatening nature of the competition and about their own mistakes. This negative self-talk is particularly destructive[2] and can even worsen their performance.

It is normal for musicians, actors and athletes to want to perform at a very high level; for athletes, there is a very clear and measurable standard to reach, such as the height of a jump in the pole vault or a particular time in a race. For artists and musicians, however, the standard is more subjective and undefined and might be judged differently by various critics. Beyond a normal desire for excellence, perfectionist musicians or actors will not only set *excessively* high standards for themselves, but they will allow *little flexibility* to make mistakes.

Sam, a pianist, is rarely satisfied with his performance. Mistakes are not seen as useful lessons from which to learn. Small errors, in his eyes, mean total failure. Because the likelihood of a less-than-perfect performance is high, he often becomes anxious and somewhat exhausted before a challenging recital even begins. Typically perfectionist musicians like Sam tend to catastrophize about their performance, fearful that it will be a disaster.

Authors Miriam Elliott and Susan Meltsner write of this fear of failure, which of course extends to perfectionists beyond musicians, actors and athletes:

> You approach each goal you set for yourself with your entire identity on the line. If you succeed, you are a hero. If you fail, you are the lowest life form on the planet. Unfortunately, because your standards for success are so high and because deep down inside you believe you do not have what it takes to succeed, the potential to fail seems to lurk around every corner and with it the prospect of feeling utterly powerless and completely inadequate. Consequently if you are a performance perfectionist, avoiding failure and the emotional uproar it creates is apt to be an even more powerful motivating force in your life than your desire to succeed.[3]

In contrast, the perfectionist who has high standards, is organized and disciplined and is able to adjust to failure *without feeling their whole identity is on the line*, will obviously often flourish in the competitive worlds of athletics, professional music, theater or dance. This is the positive side of perfectionism.

PROCRASTINATION

People procrastinate for a variety of reasons. Two of the most common reasons are laziness and perfectionism. Laziness is easy to understand. Perfectionism is a little more complex, but it is hardly surprising that if someone believes that they have to reach a particular standard on a difficult task and the probability of making mistakes and failing is high, they would keep putting off the task until they feel more confident of success.

One of my students could not hand in papers on time. He would put off working on them until the last possible minute, and by then it was too late to get them in by the deadline. Such delays in handing in papers postpone exposure to criticism, but the perfectionist feels justified because of the desire to do the best possible job. With the paper still in hand, last minute corrections or amplifications can always be made, but once it is handed in, that possibility is gone forever. If the deadline forces them to hand in the paper, then imperfections can be rationalized by blaming lack of time for further corrections. It is better to be blamed for lack of effort or efficiency than lack of ability!

The frequency of academic procrastination has been found to be associated with high parental expectations and high parental criticism. Procrastinators fear that they will not be able to live up to the expectations of others.[4] Fear of failure and perhaps subjective resistance to the requirements of the task are probably the most common reasons for procrastination. Besides the fear of failure, students with this problem tend to feel more anxious, more pessimistic and less in control of their situation.[5] Procrastinators often need help to structure a task and break it into manageable parts, each with its own deadline.

Another of my students described his internal conflict:

> I place pressure on myself to perfectly perform. . . . If I cannot meet this standard, then the effort (no matter how detailed and diligent) and the end result (no matter how excellent) are worthless. In the past, I found great enjoyment in composing an academic paper. . . . However in recent years, the pressure I place on myself to perform has stripped away any enjoyment I once received from writing. Simple papers routinely take me at least three times longer to complete than the average student. I scru-

pulously examine each word, sentence and paragraph. . . . In my mind, as I write, every paper must be worthy of publishing, each thesis worthy of a Pulitzer Prize. . . . I find it extremely difficult to accept criticism. . . . When someone critiques my work, even constructively, and finds fault with it, I feel as if their criticism is a personal attack. I become defensive, angry, resentful, and will meticulously seek to discredit the "unjust" assessment.

With such concerns and fears it is not surprising that such a person would procrastinate about writing or handing in a paper.

INDECISIVENESS

Strongly related to procrastination is the problem of indecisiveness. Research has demonstrated an association between difficulty making decisions and, what is a repeated theme in unhealthy perfectionism, excess concern about mistakes and doubt about the quality of one's actions. People who set high standards for themselves but are not too concerned about minor mistakes are more decisive.[6]

Life-changing decisions about where to live or study, who to marry or what job to take are difficult in the best of times. Perfectionists have a greater tendency to want to hang onto all options, fearful that if they move one way, they will have forever lost the chance to go the other way, so they become paralyzed in the process, forever oscillating between options and weighing consequences in their minds.

We live in a multiple-choice culture where we have to make decisions about so many more things than our parents did, whether it concerns brands of toothpaste, shampoo, cereal or cars! The increase in options and choices means that decisions require more effort and that there is a greater risk of making mistakes. In his book *The Paradox of Choice*, Barry Schwartz describes the recent research on this topic. He contrasts two types of people, "Maximizers" and "Satisficers." Maximizers, like perfectionists, "seek and accept only the best." They are nagged by doubts after making a choice and experience less satisfaction with more regret and rumination. "Satisficers settle for something that is good enough and do not worry about the possibility that there might be something better." They are "content with the merely excellent rather than the absolute best."[7] Schwartz comments, "The drawbacks of maximizing are so profound and the benefits so tenuous that we may well ask why anyone would pursue such a strategy."[8] In most decisions we have to give up one thing in order to gain another, and these tradeoffs make the perfectionist profoundly uncomfortable. The perfectionist tends to be reluctant to let go of any alternative lest they make a mistake and lose too much. When regret is anticipated, it is avoided by procrastination and sometimes paralysis.[9]

Indecisiveness is also a common feature of clinical depression.[10] It is especially marked when someone who has perfectionist or obsessional traits becomes depressed. My own areas of perfectionism were revealed at a time of great stress in my life when I had to make very difficult decisions. I felt paralyzed and terrified of making a wrong choice, and I used every possible excuse to delay a final decision. As I became bogged down in depression, even minor decisions about what to wear became difficult. Eventually, with the help and patience of my wife, kind friends, antidepressants and God, I emerged from a difficult place, humbled but wiser. Even though I have strongly recommended antidepressants to some of my clients, I still felt shame at being so "weak" that I needed medication to break the depressive thought patterns. But sometimes there is a biological vicious circle that takes over and makes thinking through things and changing perspective incredibly difficult. Our bodies and minds are intimately related to each other. In some situations the depression may have to be treated first to enable the decision to be made more rationally and less impulsively. In other situations, a difficult decision will have to be made first to enable the depression to lift.

Indecisiveness is also often associated with procrastination, obsessional thinking and compulsive checking. My client Bob came from a broken family and had been convinced that he was unlovable. He compensated for this by trying to be perfect in order to win acceptance. He dressed impeccably but took hours to decide what to wear each day. He would often check and recheck his appearance in the mirror. He was also so fearful of making mistakes and revealing flaws that he procrastinated at work and tried to avoid as many commitments as possible. This example shows that perfectionism can manifest itself not only in procrastination and indecision but also in obsessive-compulsive traits.

OBSESSIVE-COMPULSIVE PERSONALITY AND OBSESSIVE-COMPULSIVE DISORDERS

In the movie *As Good as It Gets,* Jack Nicholson illustrates a mixture of obsessive-compulsive personality and obsessive-compulsive disorder (OCD). He walks the streets of New York, avoiding cracks in the sidewalk. He wears gloves for everything. Whenever he washes his hands, he uses a new bar of soap. He eats at the same restaurant at the same time every day and makes sure he is served by the same waitress. An important difference between obsessive-compulsive personality and obsessive-compulsive disorder is that the person with OCD does not want or like their symptoms, whereas the person with obsessive-compulsive personality does not wish to be rid of their tendencies and, in fact, thinks that they are healthy and should be emulated by others. This was the case with Jack Nicholson's character. He did not seem to be distressed by many of his symptoms.*

What psychiatrists call obsessive-compulsive personality disorder is an exaggerated form of perfectionism. With OCD there are unwanted, intrusive, recurrent and often extreme thoughts and impulses that cause great anxiety. In order to reduce the anxiety, there is a strong compulsion to respond to those thoughts by performing repetitive behaviors or mental acts, though sometimes people will experience obsessive thoughts without resorting to compulsive actions. They may have obsessive doubts, fears, images or impulses. For example, a young mother might have repeated distressing thoughts that her child will be kidnapped.[11]

In my earlier psychiatric practice my colleagues and I treated a number of people who struggled with OCD. For example, Jim felt compelled to check that he had locked the door of his house thirty times before he could sleep at night. Sally plugged and unplugged electrical appliances again and again before she could use them. David felt a powerful urge to shout obscenities in public and could only suppress it by repeatedly counting backwards from fifty to one. Mary, in order to prevent infection by germs, washed her hands and arms forty times a day until they were raw. All of these people experienced great distress if they tried to resist their compulsions, becoming more and more anxious until they gave in to them. Thankfully there are behavioral therapy techniques and medications that help to break these vicious cycles, although therapy is often difficult and prolonged. OCD seems to have a strong biological basis so that it is as if there is a short circuit in particular brain connections. Medication is very helpful for many people.[12]

Randy Frost, a clinical psychologist and leading researcher on per-

---

*A severe case of OCD is illustrated in the story of Howard Hughes in the movie *The Aviator*.

fectionism, believes that perfectionism is a "necessary but not sufficient condition" for OCD. In other words, one can be a perfectionist without developing OCD, but people with OCD usually have perfectionist tendencies before the OCD becomes apparent.[13]

As obsessive tendencies become more intense in OCD there is an exaggerated sense of responsibility for reducing threat, avoiding danger and preventing illness (and death!). There is even a growing sense of omniscience and omnipotence, where the person believes that they have the power to set in motion or prevent disasters by obsessive rumination or magical rituals. Also, believing that some of their feelings and thoughts are unacceptable, they may fear some catastrophic punishment.[14] People with OCD often believe that their thoughts are just as powerful as their actions, and therefore they feel a great responsibility for thinking the "right" thoughts. When they think "wrong" thoughts they feel very guilty.

We see, in the obsessive personality and OCD, the themes of perfectionism taken to an extreme. It is clear that perfectionist thinking and behavior are attempts to avoid uncertainty and danger by not making mistakes and thus maintaining control over one's environment.[15] John's painful story will help to illustrate some of these themes.

Endless struggle and conflict. As he recalls it, his symptoms first appeared when he began grade school. He vividly remembers the intense feelings of anxiety and fear as he boarded the bus every day. He would spend the entire ride praying. Away from the security of his mother, thoughts of gloom and doom would invade his mind, like a stereo playing in the next room. He would pray loudly over the voices, drowning them out with his obsessive inner mantra. Prayer became a compulsive act, designed to counter the evil of the world. He was convinced these thoughts and voices came from the devil himself.

As the years went by the compulsive acts became intertwined with almost every facet of John's life. Obsessive thoughts and compulsive behaviors became very intense in his adolescence, peaking around the age of fourteen. Everything had to be done perfectly. Quick and easy tasks would take unbelievable amounts of time.

The simple act of taking my shoes off and setting them on the floor became a tortuous endeavor. I would hold the shoes together with my left hand, heels touching and repeatedly alternate setting them on the floor then picking them back up. I would turn them over to see the bottom of the sole then back to the floor over and over. After five to ten times, I might be able to let them go, only to look back at them feeling something just wasn't right. Then the ritual would begin again until it felt "okay." Once the shoes were secure I would next attempt to get into bed. I would sit on the edge of the bed with the covers pulled back. Both of my feet would have to leave the floor at exactly the same time as I attempted to lie down. . . . Once I managed to successfully lie down, I would begin a long involved prayer, asking for the Lord's help with anything I could imagine that could possibly harm my family or the world. Once I had asked Him for all the protection I could think of, the prayer would end. Finally I had reached my one true escape—sleep.

As John matured he began to realize that his fears were irrational and that no evil would happen if he refused the inner demands. Resisting them was very difficult at first, like "pulling a pin from a grenade and waiting for it to explode." Each day he hoped that things would be different, and each day, for many years, he was disappointed. "I have fought this version of hell on earth, to varying degrees, for the better part of my thirty-six years."

Amazingly John did not realize that he was struggling with a recognized illness, OCD. He did not talk to anyone about his troubles or seek professional help. He was too embarrassed to admit the lack of control he was feeling. Once John did begin to seek help for depression and OCD, he was greatly helped by medication, counseling, a faithful wife, and a deeper understanding of the goodness and grace of God. His marriage and family life are much improved, and he now works as a professional counselor, helping men who are trapped in the snares of addiction.

Scrupulosity and oversensitive conscience. We began to explore scrupulosity in a general way under the heading of moral perfectionism. My student Patrick told me of his struggles with it in a paper that he wrote for a class. He remembered developing perfectionist tendencies as a child. Chores and, when he was old enough, paid jobs took him longer than the average person. He paid attention to every detail of the task and was often accused of being slow because of his obsession with perfection. Working on the golf course, the cups had to be cut just right, the sand traps perfectly raked, and every single ball mark and divot in sight had to be repaired. Only under pressure to finish at a certain time could he give up and move on. In his studies, his papers were never good enough. A one-page reflection could take up to three hours. When writing a letter everything had to be by the rules. He would call someone with a question over a comma and felt uncomfortable with broad guidelines in anything. He was passionate about precision. In his moral life he strove to be utterly consistent. He wrote:

> Time clock questions drive me crazy. Was my break too long? Do I need to deduct for a conversation I had with someone? Every statement is analyzed for detecting error, every purchase for economic responsibility, every action for complete fidelity to

the rules, every confession for complete honesty, and every decision, "Was it the right one?"

The *New Catholic Encyclopedia* defines *scrupulosity* as "habitual and unreasonable hesitation, doubt, coupled with anxiety of mind, in connection with the making of moral judgments."[16] It notes that the word is derived from a Latin word meaning "a small stone," something that might lodge in one's shoe and cause acute discomfort, making each step "painful and hesitant." Psychiatrist O. Hobart Mowrer writes that the scrupulous person tends to be "excessively . . . honest" and is preoccupied with "moral trifles. . . . They are quick to label indifferent actions as sinful. . . . They worry about past confessed sins which their memories are forever dredging up."[17] The scrupulous person is never sure that he has confessed deeply, precisely or truthfully enough. He may make repeated confessions, trying to get rid of his doubts. He ruminates over decision and action, constantly worried lest he commit sin; although, to most people he appears to be functioning quite normally.†

Luther and Bunyan. It is hard for us to believe that people of great ability and intelligence, who we admire as heroes of faith, could have serious psychological struggles. Psychiatrist Gaius Davies, in a study of some famous Christians, titled *Genius, Grief and Grace,*[18] reveals that Martin Luther, John Bunyan, Gerard Manley Hopkins, J. B. Phillips and Christina Rossetti all struggled with symptoms of unhealthy perfectionism and obsessive thinking at some point in their lives. Martin Luther, in his early life in the monastery, would spend hours confessing the tiniest sins:

---

†It appears that scrupulosity is less common than it used to be, perhaps because of a diminished awareness of sin in our culture, and also because of changes in the Catholic preparation for confession.

I tried to live according to the Rule with all diligence, and I used to be contrite, to confess and number off my sins, and often repeated my confession, and sedulously performed my allotted penance. And yet my conscience could never give me certainty, but I always doubted and said, "You did not perform that correctly. You were not contrite enough. You left that out of your confession."[19]

Although many monks were preoccupied by their sin because their salvation, they believed, depended on confessing everything and living a devout and perfect life, Luther's fears were exaggerated by his perfectionist personality. The positive side of his perfectionism is seen in the outpouring of high quality writing that must have required enormous self-discipline and hard work. The foundation of the negative side of his perfectionism, his great fear of losing his salvation, was taken away when he was struck with terror as, at his very first mass, he held in his hands what he believed to be the very body and blood of Christ. How could he, a sinful mortal, be in the presence of such holiness? There he understood for the first time the amazing forgiveness and grace of God and was liberated from his fear of punishment and rejection.

Even after this transforming experience, doubt and conviction of sin troubled him. But he would challenge the devil's use of his old scrupulosity:

Sometimes it is necessary to drink a little more, play, joke, or even commit some sin in defiance and contempt of the devil in order not to give him an opportunity to make us scrupulous about small things. We will be overcome if we worry too much about falling into some sin. . . . What do you think is my reason for drinking wine undiluted, talking freely, and eating more often if it is not to torment and vex the devil who has made up his mind to torment and vex me?[20]

Luther loved to comfort troubled consciences with the message of the gospel. Some sense of his own pain and relief is seen in his comment "To raise one conscience up out of despair is worth more than a hundred kingdoms."[21]

John Bunyan, the Puritan preacher and author of *Pilgrim's Progress*, struggled with an oversensitive conscience that often condemned him,[22] and for several years he was tormented by compulsions to blaspheme when he was in the pulpit and had intense doubts about his salvation. Davies calls this the "doubting madness" and comments, "When you feel that your eternal destiny is involved, when that is your worry and not simply whether you have locked the door or turned off the gas, then the anxiety level is, by comparison, infinitely higher."[23] Bunyan was greatly helped by Luther's writings.[24]

CONCLUSION

After this long chapter you may think that I have been obsessing about the more extreme worries and fears that often torment perfectionists! However, I hope the examples I have used give a realistic picture of the struggle as well as hope that substantial, if not complete, healing is possible. In the next chapter we will explore some of the problems encountered by perfectionists in their relationships.

QUESTIONS FOR DISCUSSION

1. Athletes, musicians and other performers have to push themselves to reach very high standards. What makes the difference for them

between healthy and unhealthy perfectionism?

2. If you, like many people, tend to procrastinate, do you think there is an element of perfectionism in your thinking or behavior?

3. How would you help someone who always has a hard time making decisions because they are afraid that it will not be "the right one"?

4. How would you differentiate between a normal conscience and an excessively overactive or underactive conscience?

5. Do you suspect that the real problem for a Christian who struggles with worry, indecisiveness and excessive guilt is that they need more faith?

6

THE THOUGHT PATTERNS
OF PERFECTIONISM

All-or-nothing thinking underlies many of the features of unhealthy perfectionism. Of course, there are some things in this world that are literally black or white, as there are some things that are morally right or wrong. But there is much, especially in human relationships, that is not exactly one or the other. This fact makes life very difficult for someone who likes things clearly and concisely defined. Such a person thinks, for example, that they must do everything "just right" or not at all. They tend to see everything in polarized categories: A room is either perfectly clean and tidy or horribly dirty and chaotic; a particular course of action is absolutely bad or perfectly good. They think of themselves as either perfect saints or terrible sinners—or, at least, exceptional versus merely ordinary. Being mediocre or average is cause for contempt. In the mind of the unhealthy perfectionist, success is minimized and failure maximized. One small mistake can be quickly transformed into a massive failure. If they express anger, fear or jealousy, then they think of themselves as a terribly bad and selfish person. Other people may be idealized when things are going well but treated with derision when a flaw is discovered. At one time the perfectionist may appear arrogant and proud, at another time, profoundly humble, self-denigrating and even depressed.

One young mother described to me how she oscillates between feeling like a good mother when her children are behaving (a rare moment!) and feeling like a complete and utter failure when her children misbehave or her baby cries for too long. A student of mine once wept over the one B in a series of As. This signified to him—though, obviously, not to his professors or anyone who knew him—that he was a complete failure.

Another student summed it up very well when he wrote in a class assignment, "One manner in which perfectionism manifests itself in my life is the pressure to perfectly perceive. I tend to think in 'black and white' terms. . . . A concept or opinion is either right or wrong. There is no compromise. Therefore I feel an enormous amount of pressure to find *the* proper perspective." A preoccupation with finding the ultimate truth may lead to endless hours of philosophical discussion in an attempt to find the perfect formulation of a concept. The precise and exhaustive manner in which the perfectionist may speak is often irritating for others. Recounting events takes time as no detail is omitted. The point or conclusion of a tale may have to be drawn out by painful prodding because the perfectionist will want to cover every detail lest they be accused of being inaccurate or wrong.

Swiss psychiatrist Paul Tournier writes of all-or-nothing thinkers:

> They are so full of ambition in everything that they are always disappointed with reality and with themselves. Among them are musicians who harbor such wonderful dreams of artistic

perfection that as soon as they take up an instrument they are discouraged at falling so far short of their ambition, and they abandon their studies. These "all or nothing" types have such an intense need for affection that they have scarcely taken up acquaintance with someone when they break off relationship because they are disappointed at not finding in him what they consider to be true friendship. . . . (They) are always dreaming of being entrusted with important tasks, and meanwhile they neglect the humbler duties whose accomplishment would carry them forward. I listen to the account of many such lives: permanently provisional lives, one might call them.[1]

INTOLERANCE OF AMBIGUITY

Such black-and-white thinking leads to intolerance of ambiguity and difficulty living in the uncertainties between two points of view. Maturity in life comes from learning, often through difficult experiences, to live in balance or creative tension between the inevitable polarities of existence.

For example, in order to feel safe, some perfectionists may try to dominate and take control, making things happen the way they want. Other perfectionists may swing to the opposite extreme, and if they cannot be in total control, they will become very passive and dependent. They will often feel totally responsible for something or reject responsibility completely. Trying to live between these extremes creates a lot of tension. It leads to contradictory tendencies as the person oscillates from one pole of thinking to the other.

Here is another very confusing aspect of perfectionism: the desire to be certain and the dislike of ambiguity and ambivalence are accompanied by a fear of commitment to any opinion. Perfectionists therefore find themselves trapped in the situation of trying to avoid ambivalence, but the fear of making mistakes actually produces it. They may swing between extremes of absolute opinions and pervasive doubts.

Most of us prefer a simple formula for progress and success in life. Parents want a recipe that will guarantee a perfectly behaved child or teenager. Christians want a formula for the happy and successful life. We are attracted to rules and recipes because they seem to remove uncertainty and ambiguity in life. Unfortunately—and perfectionists feel this tension acutely—life is not so clean cut and tidy. Raising secure and confident children depends not just on a set of rules; instead, it hinges on relationships that are less easily defined and on applying principles to each child's different personality. This lack of exactness creates insecurity in the perfectionist.

Similarly, in the church, although there are many aspects of Christian teaching that are clear and unambiguous, there are some aspects of reality that have to be held in tension. For example: law and grace, God's sovereignty and our responsibility, justice and mercy, predestination and freewill, and doctrine and experience. Perfectionists, more than most, find it hard to live in tension or balance between two complimentary and parallel truths. As a result, they are often attracted to legalistic churches where they are clearly told what to believe on every issue and where there are clearly prescribed ways of dressing and behaving. They know exactly where they stand, and this makes them feel secure.

Some perfectionists are preoccupied with structure and order. Quite often they find the "just hanging loose" and "going with the flow" attitude of the nonperfectionist very frightening and anxiety provoking. An extreme reaction to this fear of loss of control is seen in obsessive-compulsive disorder, in which checking and washing rituals ensure everything is done "just right."

RIGIDITY AND RESISTANCE TO CHANGE

We all vary in our ability to adjust to new and unfamiliar ideas, situations or surroundings. Perfectionists like things to be ordered and predictable, and change is particularly stressful. Often perfectionists find it difficult to shift from one activity to another as changing situations may demand.[2] They become easily flustered and irritated and may remove themselves from a situation in order to calm their anxiety. Because of their all-or-nothing thinking, when they do desire change, it is difficult to tolerate if it is slow and gradual; the goal needs to be achieved immediately or not at all.

TYRANNY OF OUGHTS AND SHOULDS

There are some legitimate obligations and things we *ought* to do in life, but some people cannot relax and enjoy life because they are always feeling driven to do more. Their thoughts might run a bit like this: "I *should* be able to get straight As in graduate school, be a good parent to my children, get daily exercise, care for my friends in trouble, be involved with the church, take care of my house . . . without feeling too stressed by it." With the expectation that one *should* be perfect, any flaw is evidence of being a hopeless failure. One young man said to me: "I should have a neat house and a clean car. Good people have neat houses and clean cars. It's the way things ought to be." Failure produces guilt and a powerful sense that they *should* not have to repeat this same mistake again.

Unhealthy perfectionists tend to have very sensitive and sometimes distorted consciences. They often feel acute pangs of guilt or shame if they do not live up to their own, or others', expectations. Fear about what others will think about their decisions and actions becomes their central concern. A student of mine wrote the following:

I am often overcome with the desire to perfectly please. I am frequently more motivated by my desire to receive acceptance and praise from other people . . . than by the simple pursuit of excellence. . . . My family moved frequently when I was a child. Every time I changed schools, I lost a group of friends and was forced to find new ones. I thought that the best way to make friends was to please people around me. . . . Even now I battle feelings of social inferiority, never feeling that I can measure up to the imagined expectations I presume others have of me, and fearing that if I fail to meet these expectations, I will be viewed as an abhorrent outcast.

In order to feel safe and acceptable this woman's life was dominated by attempts to live by what she imagined others thought she *ought* to be or do. She did not really know who she was or what she wanted for herself. In her fear of failure and rejection she was constantly trying to avoid guilt and shame.

FEAR OF MAKING MISTAKES

We have repeatedly seen that one of the results of wanting everything to be predictable, safe, controlled and "right" is a huge fear of making mistakes—of one's fallibility and weakness being exposed for all to see. Decisions, especially big ones such as whom to marry or what career to pursue, can be hard at the best of times for anyone. For perfectionists, such decisions can be exquisitely painful because they are always accompanied by indecision and gnawing doubt. The motto of the perfectionist in this area might be "nothing ventured, nothing lost." Perfectionists don't take risks for fear of getting it wrong. This anxiety is so strong that it makes responsible decisions and any kind of moral action almost impossible. Action will be postponed again and again while more information is gathered to help make the "right" decision. Fear of making the wrong decision makes it difficult to give up any options that are available. Paul Tournier says that perfectionists "want to do everything, but choose nothing, and so never get started. Living means choosing one thing rather than another, but these people will give up nothing, and so lose everything."[3]

There is a fear of commitment because a decision settled on might be wrong, and then the perfectionist will have to deal with the uncomfortable emotions of disappointment, guilt and shame, and in life-changing decisions, a frightening awareness of our lack of control over our own fate.

For Christians, believing that they should ask for God's help, there can be a temptation to avoid the hard work of decision making by procrastinating and giving the high sounding reason that we are "waiting on the Lord." Dennis Gibson writes:

> "Seeking God's will." "The leading of the Lord." "God is able." These words readily degenerate into cliches that justify indecision. It is easier for us to say we are "waiting on the Lord" than to complete the hard work of making a decision that has costs as well as benefits. Our obsessive tendencies shrink from commitments. Our religious language offers us a sacred sounding smoke screen for cowardice. We "put out the fleece" instead of using our best judgment, deciding, and learning from any painful consequences that ensue. We resist trial and error learning, which happens to be one of God's favorite ways to teach us wisdom. In order to get on with life we must take a stand, letting go of some of the alternatives available to us. Our obsessive desire to be masters of our fate insists on keeping all options open lest we make a mistake. In this process we sacrifice joy on the altar of control.[4]

ATTRACTION TO LEGALISM

As I mentioned earlier in the chapter, perfectionists are often attracted to legalism because they like structure and clear judgments on all issues in life. Legalistic churches, in their honest zeal to promote faithfulness and obedience to God, plainly define the rules and codes of conduct that they expect their members to adhere to. This usually goes way beyond major biblical principles to address minor issues of how one should dress in church, whether one drinks alcohol and other concerns that are not central to Christian belief.

Legalistic churches and their leaders tend to be authoritarian. The pastor, the elders or the church council, believing that they are guardians of the truth and the law of God, often govern with a firm hand, allowing little freedom for congregational involvement in decisions. Leaders in the church do not have an easy task at the best of times, but where there is a tendency to legalism, fear and guilt are usually the chief means of control.

Members of legalistic churches leave the sermon each week tending to feel considerable guilt, with a heavy burden to try harder and do better. They often think that if they keep to the formula—daily "quiet time" with God, regular church attendance, involvement with church programs and no drinking—then God will be satisfied.

This too happens in legalistic and authoritarian families. Matters such as dress or length and style of hair become important moral issues, often creating enormous tension between parents and children. Bruce Narramore, in an article on parental discipline and the necessity of grace, discusses such legalistic parenting:

> If they [parents] follow principles of law they will focus on external conformity, demand a certain level of performance before

they approve their children, withhold blessings until they are satisfied with their child's achievements, punish for misbehavior, and rely on fear as a major motivation. In short, they . . . will operate more as judges or policemen in their relations with their children.[5]

The Pharisees in the New Testament were extreme legalists (moral perfectionists), creating hundreds of little regulations and rules beyond the Ten Commandments. They believed that only those who kept all the rules would be acceptable to God. Jesus commented that, although they were excellent at tithing a tenth of their produce, they had neglected the more important issues of "justice, mercy and faithfulness" (Mt 23:23). They had all the external marks of religiosity but lacked sincere love for God and others.

Any kind of legalism tends to apply biblical principles in hard and uncompassionate ways, where there is little room for weakness, failure or grace. By contrast, the message of the gospel is that all of us, parents and pastors included, are in constant need of God's help, grace and forgiveness.[6]

DENIAL OF REALITY

In some areas the unhealthy or neurotic perfectionist has lost touch with reality. I was taught as a medical student that "neurotics build castles in the air, psychotics live in them, and psychiatrists collect the rent!" In other words, neurotics have a dream of how they want their life to be, psychotics live in the dream they believe is real, and psychiatrists get paid to treat them. We are all, to some degree, neurotic because we can be unrealistic about ourselves, others and the world. The more neurotic we are, the more we believe that we can and should be able to reach our ideal.

Psychologist Abraham Maslow believed that there are two fundamentally different motivations for living. The healthy perfectionist is motivated by the possibility of growth and knows that it will take time, whereas the neurotic perfectionist is motivated by a sense of deficiency and urgency to be a different person *now*.[7]

W. S. Taylor, quoting psychoanalyst Karen Horney, writes of the perfectionists' inadequate grasp of the relationship between means and ends, of their "disregard for the feasibility of achieving their goal."[8] In their efforts to live out their idealized pictures of the world, neurotic perfectionists tend to telescope the whole process involved in realizing their objectives, treating the end result as though it were the next step and dropping the intermediate links.

It is hard for perfectionists to acknowledge shortcomings because they may experience enormous shame and self-contempt. In order to avoid these feelings, they have to distort reality, deny personally deviant behavior and present themselves "in the best possible light."[9] This becomes a vicious circle as they then feel shame for lying.

Denial and distortion of reality. This is strong language! But, to one degree or another, we all find parts of reality hard to accept. We all find ways to avoid things we find uncomfortable and threatening. The perfectionist is in danger of doing this in a way that, in the long run, is very damaging.

CONCLUSION

Thus far I have examined the nature of perfectionism, some problems that arise from unhealthy perfectionism and, in this chapter, the underlying thought patterns of perfectionism. In the next few chapters we will be looking at several different roots of perfectionism.

QUESTIONS FOR DISCUSSION

1. Do you see yourself as an all-or-nothing thinker?

2. Why do perfectionists have a hard time with change?

3. Mistakes are surely not good! So why is fear of mistakes such a problem?

4. What do you understand about legalism? Do you see examples of this in your family, church, school or work?

5. How are some perfectionists out of touch with, or in denial of, reality?

7

GENES AND TEMPERAMENT

There are many different factors that contribute to the development of perfectionism. There are some children who, at a very young age, are particularly concerned about cleanliness, tidiness and order. This pattern seems to be hardwired into their brains because it emerges very early in life, before parents could have contributed much to this development. However, either a parent's reaction will reinforce the perfectionism so that it becomes unhealthy, or it will help the child learn to deal with their predisposition in a healthier manner.

One mother, while acknowledging that she was a perfectionist and that her husband was "highly structured," told me that, as a gymnastics coach, she is "surrounded by perfectionists." She began to notice that when her daughter was between eighteen months and two years old, the child would "have a temper tantrum because her Poptart had a crack in it; start an argument with a friend who put a toy away incorrectly; and express anger at just about anything which she could not accomplish alone." It is impossible to say how much of this child's perfectionism is inherited versus learned from her parents. However, a consistent and repeated comment from some parents that their children have an excessive concern about cleanliness and neatness at a very early age makes me suspect a genetic component. The little research that has been done on childhood perfectionism found that "high fearfulness" and "high levels of persistence" may be predisposing temperamental characteristics.[1]

Psychologists Kenneth Rice and Karen Preusser have developed a test for measuring perfectionism in children called the Adaptive/Maladaptive Perfectionism Scale (AMPS). They developed this with nine- to eleven-year-olds and found that four factors stood out above others. The more perfectionist children had more "sensitivity to making mistakes" and had difficulty accepting less-than-perfect work. Their sense of self-esteem was strongly linked to parental approval or rejection ("contingent self-esteem"). They had a strong "need for admiration" in order to feel good about themselves. Finally, they were "compulsive" in their need for order, organization and task completion.[2]

I asked friends and students if they noticed some of these characteristics in their own children, and they gave me a number of examples: A two-and-a-half-year-old with two fairly perfectionist parents insists that his "blankie" be laid on him vertically and *not* horizontally. One four-year-old always wants to dress very neatly, and if the sock she is putting on is twisted around the wrong way, she will have a tantrum. Both parents had strong perfectionist tendencies and of course found it difficult to be patient with an imperfect child!

It is important to note, especially for the sake of anxious parents, that children between the ages of two and four are more prone to abnormal fears and desires for sameness and symmetry than older children. They may demand certain bedtime routines and develop all sorts of superstitions and checking rituals to ward off danger. These will pass as the child grows, and they should not be a cause of concern unless they persist. But there are some children who do seem, from a very early age, to have a perfectionist streak.

There may be phases of perfectionist, obsessive behavior in older children. Some of this is probably genetic, and some may be a reaction to insecurity. Mary, a student, told me about a time between the ages of seven and thirteen when she classified everything as either "clean" or "dirty." She recalled,

> I distinguished areas of the floors in our house as clean and dirty. I divided our car into a clean and dirty side. Worst of all, I placed people in these categories. I think this might have been based on smells and/or the individual's level of tidiness. My piano teacher, I remember, had a very distinct unpleasant smell, so I thought of her as "dirty" and would always wash my hands after the lesson. Sometime I stopped obsessing about cleanliness, and by about thirteen years of age, I think there was nothing left of my "clean" and "dirty" system. In fact, I had nearly forgotten this altogether until one night when my husband told me I was obsessively cleaning the house. Then I told him about the system I used as a child and we both laughed about it.

Mary told me that her mother is a fastidious housekeeper, but otherwise there are hardly any traits of perfectionism in her family. None of her siblings were as concerned about neatness or cleanliness as she was.

So we find that the perfectionist personality traits that we have seen in adults are also present in some children from a very early age. In others they emerge through childhood and adolescence. As the examples above demonstrate, it is difficult to distinguish between a genetic predisposition, a learned behavior and a normal developmental phase. However, perfectionist personality traits are partly inborn and partly learned, which testifies to the amazing complexity of human beings and the interwoven influences of nature and nurture.

One key aspect of perfectionism is sensitivity to making mistakes. This is closely linked to shame and guilt, which is an important and somewhat complex topic that needs to be unpacked in more detail in the next chapter before we can see its relationship to perfectionism. You may not immediately see its relevance, but be patient with me. The practical implications will be seen in chapter ten.

QUESTIONS FOR DISCUSSION

1. Many children show some perfectionist traits. Do you know of children who had perfectionist traits from a very early age and for whom this was not just a phase of normal development (i.e., they did not outgrow it) but an ongoing personality style?

2. Do you agree with the idea that perfectionism may be partly genetic in origin?

8

SHAME AND GUILT

One of the most powerful driving forces behind perfectionism is shame. This is a complex emotion that has a close relationship to guilt. In fact, the two are often interwoven and mistaken for one another. It is important to spend a little time trying to distinguish between guilt and shame, and between appropriate and inappropriate shame.

I am aware that my readers will not necessarily share my Christian worldview, of which I have only given hints of so far, but in discussing guilt and shame, I cannot avoid the importance of belief about the source of moral values. I hope that you will, at least, stay with me to see where we can agree, and perhaps consider the possibility of the relevance and truth of Christianity in dealing with perfectionism. I will assume some familiarity with the more well-known stories of the Bible since I will be using these as examples.

DISCERNING BETWEEN GUILT AND SHAME

Imagine your conscience is like a smoke detector with two different tones that warn you when something is wrong and corrective action needs to be taken. It is what I will call a "guilt and shame detector." Both guilt and shame are built-in systems of self-evaluation arising from our consciences. Most people have not learned to discriminate between the two and so hear only one tone. But when our consciences are functioning correctly we can learn to recognize two separate tones, one for guilt and one for shame. Sometimes they go off together; sometimes they are triggered separately. It is very important to know the difference, because the remedy is different for each.

In a world where there is a God who defines a particular moral order, guilt is not just a feeling; it is a fact—the signal of having done something wrong, of having offended our Creator. Guilt is the conscious awareness of this reality, which is acknowledged in confession and repentance and removed by forgiveness.[1] Author Dick Keyes, in his book *Beyond Identity,* makes a helpful distinction: If guilt is felt in relation to morals (what I *do*), then shame is felt in relation to models—who I *am* in relation to who I think I ought to *be.*[2] One is about actions or thoughts, the other about the very nature of my being and character. At its most simple, guilt says, "I have done something wrong"; shame says, "I am a bad person."

Shame is an experience of being a dishonorable, inferior or worthless person. Shame results from failing to live up to expectations: our own, other people's or God's. It is usually triggered when we anticipate disapproval or rejection, and when our foolishness, weakness or sin is exposed.

An embarrassing situation. One night I was eating dinner with my wife and daughter. My wife was showing me some landscaping drawings for our church that she had just paid to have done. I reached for the salt and accidentally knocked over a glass of water. Horrified, I watched as the water poured over the waxed paper and the detailed drawing flowed off the paper onto the table, disappearing in a gray puddle. My immediate feeling was an overwhelming sense of shame at my foolishness. How could I be such a klutz? Would my wife ever respect her clumsy husband again? I longed for her to say something reassuring: "Oh, I know you didn't mean to do it, my dear!" But there was no such reassurance. I could see her stony face out of the corner of my eye and could not look at her. I avoided her direct gaze, which I knew would only confirm my stupidity. I wanted her to hug me and to look at me with love in her eyes, but she was dealing with her own feelings of anger and frustration. She did well because she said nothing!

I thought I deserved her contempt and anger, but I also knew that I had not intended to spill the water. Of course, I should have been more careful. While I did not feel guilt, I clearly felt shame. As we cleared up the mess, I apologized profusely, and at last (it felt like a week, but it was only a few minutes) she spoke: "It's OK. I think we may be able to salvage something, and I know you didn't mean to!" Then she looked at me and smiled. It was that sense of acceptance and restoration of relationship that washed away the shame. I did not need forgiveness. I needed acceptance with all my foolishness and clumsiness!

APPROPRIATE GUILT AND SHAME?

I believe that we live in a moral universe where our Creator has given us his instructions for how we can best live in his world. The commandments are not there to make our lives miserable but to guide us into living with the greatest freedom in God's world. These laws are deeply embedded in our minds, in what we call our consciences. The Bible says they are "written on our hearts" (Rom 2:15). When we do break God's laws, we are objectively guilty and should feel guilt. The more we ignore or repress our guilt and shame, the more insensitive our consciences become.

In the biblical story of King David, it took a while for him to acknowledge his terrible wrongdoing after committing adultery with Bathsheba and having her husband murdered (2 Sam 11). It is extraordinary that he could repress his guilt for months, but he was eventually exposed by the prophet Nathan's cunning parable (2 Sam 12:1-13). Psalm 51 is David's moving and poetic confession. He acknowledges his guilt and expresses appropriate shame at the public disgrace and loss of honor. God forgave his sins and removed his guilt. His shame was dealt with in knowing that God had not rejected him—a finite, weak, human being, prone to folly and sin. Today, when many people no longer believe in God or absolute values, there is little real guilt but much shame at failing to live up to our models.

Shame from failure to live up to models of appearance or performance. To use Dick Keyes's helpful concept, shame arising from failing to live up to models—sometimes literal fashion models—is usually inappropriate. For example, one may feel shame for not being as beautiful as the models in *Vogue* or for not having a body like the men in *Men's Health*. Children are shamed by the models or ideals of their peer group, when they are teased for being fat, skinny, bat-eared or clumsy. Author Anne Lamott describes her childhood experience well:

> All I ever wanted was to belong, to wear that hat of belonging.
>
> In seventh and eighth grades I still weighed about forty pounds. I was twelve years old and had been getting teased about my strange looks for most of my life. This is difficult in— the United States of Advertising, as Paul Krassner puts it—and if you are too skinny or too tall or dark or weird or short or frizzy or homely or poor or nearsighted, you get crucified. I did.[3]

These examples are all about appearance, but shame is also felt when we cannot live up to our models or inner ideals of performance. In my clumsiness I failed to live up to my own ideal of being a perfectly competent and good husband. Whether it is intelligence, athleticism or musical ability, we feel shame when we think we don't measure up.

Our families, churches or communities may have particular models of dress, behavior or suitable occupations, and when we fail to live up to those, we may feel shame. The values we put on appearance or performance vary according to the family, school or social subculture in which we live. We are not morally bound to live by them, but they have enormous influence in shaping our "smoke detectors" to feel inappropriate guilt and shame.

An upside-down world. The human heart and conscience can get so distorted that there are even some situations where morality is turned on its head. For example, if a high school or college student mixes with "bad" company for a while, he may come to feel shame for not being "man enough" to get drunk or use drugs. In many public schools, hard working and bright students are humiliated for doing well in exams or laughed at for being "religious" or "moral." A gang member may feel shame for being too cowardly to lie, cheat, steal, be promiscuous or even kill. Shame is felt not for doing something obviously wrong and harmful but for not doing it. Human consciences, our smoke detectors, can be reset by being constantly ignored or silenced. In these examples, shame works against true morality; values are inverted.

The opposite problem arises when people have very tender and oversensitive consciences. This is a particular problem for perfectionists who may be too aware of their faults and weaknesses, too scrupulous about the smallest mistake, and who always feel condemned.

That built-in sense of right and wrong ("the law of God on our hearts") is easily reinforced or distorted by parents, peers and culture, and it may need to be retrained (the smoke detector reset to be more or less sensitive) so that we learn to deal with guilt and shame in a healthy manner.

Shame from abuse. Another form of inappropriate shame is brought on those whose human dignity has been attacked by verbal, physical or sexual abuse. Here are two painful stories that describe the roots of the most damaging forms of shame and some of their effects.

Peter recognized his struggle with perfectionism and came to me for some help. His high standards, meticulous integrity and control of his emotions when under pressure stood him in good stead in the business world. In turn, he was very successful. But when he had young children he began to be aware of a deep rage inside him that, at times, threatened to break loose with frightening power.

His story slowly emerged as we met week by week. It was hard for him to talk about his very painful memories of violent abuse at the hands of his grandmother and mother, but it was important to do so in order to understand how much his thinking today had been shaped by his reactions to those early years. His father was a long-distance truck driver, and because his job required that he be away from home quite often, he did not seem to be aware of what was happening to his son. In order to survive each day, Peter had to develop a way of coping with the unpredictable dangers that lurked around every corner at home. At school he was safe. There he used his intelligence to get straight A's and keep out of trouble. From a very young age, Peter would go to school, even in the hottest weather, in long pants and a long-sleeve shirt to hide the bruises and marks. Both there and at home he tried to be the perfect child, believing that if he were good enough, the cruelty would stop.

When he returned from school each day, though, he could never tell what was going to happen. His grandmother, who lived with them and whom Peter described as the "most evil person I have ever known," might have been hiding behind the door. She would grab him and, with his mother's help, would hold his head under water in the bathtub until he was convinced he was going to die. Moments later they would pull him out, just in time. On other days, he would be beaten with an iron bar or some other implement. There was absolutely no affection or positive attention from his mother or grandmother. Peter was convinced his father knew what was going on but that he never lifted a hand or raised a voice to stop it. His other grandparents offered shelter and escape, so he would attempt to spend as much time as possible with them. When they tried to intervene, shots were fired (literally), and they were told to keep out of it. He felt intense shame for just being alive; any anger was either locked inside or directed against himself for not being good enough. As so many children do, Peter felt responsible for his mother's and grandmother's anger, as if it was his fault, as if he deserved the abuse. Just as his shame and sense of responsibility drove him to aim for perfection at school and at home, they also became the subconscious driving force for his perfectionism as an adult.

Suzan's parents were very busy in their work, and there was often tension between them. They gave her little time or attention but had high expectations of their only daughter. Suzan had always enjoyed the attention she got from her fun-loving uncle who lived nearby and who had a daughter the same age. Suzan was ten when he first began to touch her inappropriately, and he continued to abuse her for two years before abruptly moving away. She was devastated—having been seduced by him, she was now completely abandoned. What confusing feelings he created in this victim of his selfish lust: shame and guilt because she knew it was wrong; shame because she enjoyed his attention, touch and affection; shame at her own desire and her developing body, which she believed had caused him to be attracted to her.

In order to compensate for these feelings, she tried desperately to be good at everything so that other people would never find out how bad she really was. Her perfectionism was born out of her desire to hide her shame. Now she felt like "damaged goods" and unfit for any close or intimate relationship. Dan Allender states that shame is "the terror that if our dark soul is discovered we will never be enjoyed, nor desired, nor pursued by anyone."[4] This child, in her longing to belong to someone, now had a dark secret and would have a difficult time ever trusting anyone again.

It is not difficult to see how shame leads to hiding and pretense. Our instinctive reaction when any shame is exposed is to try to cover up—whether it be nakedness, mistakes, ignorance, incompetence or past sexual abuse. And because shame is an uncomfortable experience, we often deal with it in the wrong way by denial, perfectionism, anger or depression.

CONCLUSION

I hope you have stayed with me as I have attempted to find the strands of the complex knot of shame and guilt, with a particular emphasis on shame. I have focused on three types of shame: appropriate shame with true moral guilt, inappropriate shame from failing to live up to models and ideals of appearance or performance, and shame from abuse. In the next chapter we will continue to explore the roots of shame and its relationship to perfectionism.

QUESTIONS FOR DISCUSSION

1. Have you ever thought about the difference between guilt and shame?

2. In what situations have you felt shame about your appearance or performance?

3. Has your conscience been distorted in any way by your family or cultural values?

4. Do you think there are any absolute values in the universe so that there is real and appropriate guilt when we fail to keep to those standards?

5. Have you ever experienced shame from any type of abuse? How did it make you feel about yourself?

6. In what situations (if any) have you experienced true and appropriate guilt and shame at the same time?

9

PARENTAL INFLUENCES

As I have shown, parental expectations have a profound impact, often producing shame. J. Paul Getty Jr., a billionaire philanthropist, struggled with drug addictions and failed marriages. Many speculate that his problems may have had their roots in his relationship with his father, oil tycoon J. Paul Getty Sr. Raised by his mother, the younger Getty rarely saw his father. He remembered a time in high school when he wrote his father a letter, and it was returned with no personal comment and with all the spelling and grammatical errors corrected.[1] John F. Kennedy's father, Joseph, pushed his sons toward excellence and achievement and usually found something to criticize when his sons did not take first place. This ambition was epitomized by his remark "For the Kennedy's, it's the [outhouse] or the castle—nothing in between."[2]

PARENTAL INTERACTION

The most powerful people in our lives are those who care for us from the moment we are conceived, through the early years of life, and into adolescence and adulthood. Their moods, looks, words, gestures and touches convey myriad messages as to whether or not we are acceptable and loved. Then each of us has our own particular temperament that reacts, from our earliest years, in a particular way to our parents' temperaments. It is this subtle interaction that shapes our emotional and psychological life.

I spend many of my days listening to people's stories. It is a great privilege but often a sad and painful experience. Let me give you a glimpse into the lives of several people where shame was obviously imposed by thoughtless or abusive parents. I remember one mother I worked with saying to her seven-year-old, "I cannot stand you. I wish you were not my child." I think of a young man whose father wanted him to be a football player and was deeply ashamed of his son's artistic and nonathletic temperament. The young man, sensitive and musically gifted, was a profound disappointment to his father, and he eventually found the acceptance and affirmation that he longed for in a homosexual relationship. This, of course, only reinforced his father's rejection.

Trust and shaming. David, one of my students, told me of a powerful early memory. He thinks he was three years old when his father came home from work with a large bucket of ice cream. After David badgered his father for a while, his father finally told him that it was ice cream and handed him a large spoon. Little David plunged the spoon into the bucket and then into his mouth. The bucket was not full of ice cream. It was fat. It was a large bucket of cooking fat. David said, "My father got a good laugh from this practical joke, but all I can remember was shame." The "can o' lard and a big spoon" was a story told for many years, only reinforcing the shame. Events such as these were not common in his house, and David continued: "Whatever possessed him to play such a cruel trick on an unsuspecting child is

beyond me. . . . That day my father undermined my trust in a huge
way. If I could not trust my father I was certain I could not trust other
adults or even God himself."

I suspect that this father had no idea of the effect of his little joke
on his sensitive son. He probably saw it as a good game. But when
trust in a relationship is undermined at an early age, a child will tend
to protect himself from the pain of shame. As the child grows he will
learn to control emotions and, perhaps, other people to make sure
such an experience of humiliation and shame is never felt again. This
style of living and relating may continue into adult life where two
core issues of perfectionism—his desire for acceptance and the need
to be in control—will be powerful motives.

Acceptance and overcompensation. Greta was a student whose
mother's expectations were unreasonable because they were a product
of her own insecurities and perfectionism. Greta's mother focused her
obsessive efforts at control on house cleaning—it was vital that the
house be kept meticulous at all times. Friends and family were never
invited over because it would be too much trouble cleaning up after
them. While Greta obediently completed lists of household chores, she
never did them well enough to meet her mother's approval. Their most
frequent conflicts revolved around household duties, and Greta consistently faced a variety of verbal attacks. She was called "fat, lazy, in-
considerate and self-centered." Although she was certain these accusa-
tions were not true, the constant verbal slayings took their toll, and she
internalized her mother's harsh, critical voice. She directed her efforts
at things she could control in her life—she became the perfect student
and, through anorexia and bulimia, tried to achieve the perfect weight.

Greta longed to be loved and accepted, but her parents were too
preoccupied with themselves to be able to meet their daughter's deep
longings. She told me:

Mom's "occupied" sign said "I'm too tired or too obsessed with cleaning to really notice you." Dad's "occupied" sign said "I'm too depressed and beaten down to give you any time or emotional energy." Despite my active involvement in high school sports, a musical and various organizations, my parents came to only one function during my high school years. Although it was difficult for me to ask, I would often let Dad know of my next tennis or volleyball match, secretly hoping he would come. He never did. Despite my 4.0 GPA, Mom was never able to congratulate me.

HYPERCRITICAL PARENTS

We have seen how perfectionist parents often teach their children to be perfectionist, both in the way they model relationships and in the way they cope with life—their high expectations of themselves and their high expectations of their children.[3] Perfectionist parents tend to have three particularly dangerous predispositions. First, they may be intolerant of mistakes and therefore strongly critical of themselves and their children. A child who accidentally spills a glass of orange juice at the table may be castigated with, "You *stupid* child. How could you be so clumsy? You are *always* spilling things." There is no patience with genuine mistakes, and there is the implied expectation of perfect behavior. When an accident results in an attack on one's dignity and character, there is a deep sense of being a bad person and hence much shame. Second, perfectionist parents may have great difficulty showing affection and giving approval, often because they have not had much themselves. "Affectionless control" is the term used by some psychologists for the combination of high expectations and lack of warmth.[4] Third, perfectionist parents have a tendency to make acceptance conditional on performance or appearance. If children do not come very close to the top of the class, they may not be accepted. When they get seven As and one B, the B is noticed and commented on disapprovingly. Often this is because the parents' self-esteem is tied up with having a successful child—the child's success or failure becomes the parents' success or failure.

ALCOHOLISM AND DIVORCE

When a family is very dysfunctional, such as those with histories of abuse or alcoholism, where there is confusion, insecurity and unpredictability, the child may develop his or her own reactive security mechanisms to preserve some sense of order and equilibrium. Unhealthy perfectionism has often been described as one of the effects of parental alcoholism on children.[5] Similar results occur in any family where there is insecurity and uncertainty for a prolonged period of time.

Petra grew up with an alcoholic father, and she never knew how he was going to react to her. One day he would be raging and abusive, the next day sweet and tender. She hated it when he was upset and always thought it was her fault. Now when she senses someone is upset with her or disagrees with her views, she gets anxious and fearful, becomes paralyzed and has to stop the discussion. On the other hand, she has a perfectionist desire to keep things under control, and this is expressed through her strong opinions and the need to persuade others to see things as she sees them. "This strong need for control," she told me one day, "also comes from playing the role of parent as a child. I am the oldest of three siblings. This role meant that I had to keep order in the home while my dad was out drinking and my mom was at work."

Another young woman's parents divorced when she was two years old, and after the divorce she was aware of the tension between her parents whenever they communicated. She said:

> I longed for a peace between them that would never be. And yet
> somehow I was determined to bring peace and stability wher-
> ever possible in my life, possibly to compensate for the lack of
> security I felt. I became somewhat effective at this by learning
> how to please those people who could cause pain and chaos. I
> could achieve this by conforming my behavior to what was de-
> sired of me or by manipulating a situation in order to prevent
> confrontation. . . . The ultimate issue is an attempt to control
> my world as much as possible in order to prevent painful expe-
> riences.

This perfectionist style of relating was an effective protection and
worked well for her as a small child, but as an adult it makes relationships complicated and difficult. The crux of the issue, she continued,
is this:

> To some degree, I believe I can be my own god by manipulating
> my world in a way that brings fulfillment and joy in life inde-
> pendent of God. And if I can do this for myself, supposedly,
> then it only seems logical that others can do this for themselves
> with the right guidance (from me!).

She expects a lot of herself and others, and the reality and depth of
her relationships is hindered by her strong desire for peace, stability
and order.

PARENTING STYLES

The classic study by Baumrind in 1971 identified three styles of
parenting: authoritarian, permissive and authoritative.[6] At first
glance it might be easy to confuse authoritarian and authoritative,

but they are very different. Authoritarian parents tend to be overcontrolling, highly punitive and restricting, which often produces extremes of conformity or rebellion in their children. In contrast, permissive parents appear not to be very involved with their children and to set few boundaries. This often produces insecurity, a sense of shame at not being worthy of attention, and a reactive desire to please and be perfect in an attempt to avoid complete rejection. The most successful style of parenting is the authoritative, in which there is demonstrable love and involvement combined with firm boundaries and consequences. Reasonable explanations of limits are given in a setting of respect and warmth.[*]

MANY ROOTS

Very often perfectionism results from many roots—a combination of inherited temperamental factors, family example and expectations, cultural pressures, and shaming or abuse that accumulates and is compounded over the years. As an example, let me introduce you to Alice, a woman in her forties, who clearly demonstrates a combination of influences in her life. She tells her own story:

> Firstly, I have an inborn temperament towards perfectionism, truly inherited from my parents. Secondly, my parents are excellent perfectionist role models. My father is extremely intelligent and creative and quite accomplished at anything he does. If he does not know how to do something, he will teach himself

---

[*]One study described two types of learning goals that parents typically have for their children: parents with the "learning-goal orientation" emphasize understanding the material, enjoying learning and seeking challenges. In contrast, parents with the "performance-goal orientation" stress the external marks of success: grades and test scores. The latter is more likely to produce unhealthy perfectionism. See Carol S. Dweck, "Motivational Processes Affecting Learning," *American Psychologist* 41 (1986): 1040-48; Carol S. Dweck and Ellen L. Leggett, "A Social-Cognitive Approach to Motivation and Personality," *Psychological Review* 95 (1988): 256-73.

and become proficient in it. He finished our basement into a living area in his spare time when I was a child. It took two years, though, because he meticulously cut and pieced together different types of wood scraps to make a mosaic pattern of paneling for the walls. I grew up thinking all men could be plumbers, electricians, carpenters, craftsmen, mathematicians, writers, artists, high school tutors, computer experts and "perfect" men. Unfortunately my husband had a few rough years as I learned the fallacy of this expectation.

My mother, as the middle child of fourteen children raised during the Depression, grew up in insecurity, uncertainty and crowded chaos. She seems to have sought security by controlling and ordering all things. I watched my mother compulsively clean our home, trying to undo the disorder that followed in the wake of her five active children (four of them boys). She actually stripped and waxed all the wooden floors weekly. Today she can make me feel guilty (and angry) when she reprimands me for not cleaning the inside of my refrigerator weekly. It is obvious both my parents modeled a perfectionist work ethic. To this day I find it difficult to relax until all tasks and chores are finished.

Thirdly, I also have a dysfunctional religious background. My father dropped out of Christianity, probably because he could not achieve the perfection his denomination demanded, and my mother remains a staunch secular Catholic. Thus my primary religious background is a works-oriented Catholicism. Both my parents and religion harshly judged my mistakes. Indeed, I still find it difficult to admit mistakes or errors.

Additionally, I had three mischievous older brothers who were often willful and disobedient. I observed my father's anger and mother's tears in reaction to their sons' errors. I may have subconsciously tried to be the model child and earn love and attention through development of my perfectionist tendencies, as seen in my sense of organization and intense application to schoolwork. Also, the gifts and skills God has blessed me with meant I had few challenges until high school, and even these challenges were mastered with a little effort. The first time I truly faced my inability to control and master life was at age eighteen, when I received a speeding ticket for driving 32 in a 25 mile per hour residential zone. I was shamed and crushed at this imperfection, which I interpreted as [total] failure for many years.

This account illustrates the subtle interweaving of temperament, role models, unhelpful religious influences and her own self-protective choices. Alice's parents were well meaning and conscientious. They were not abusive or cruel, but their influence was still profound.

CONCLUSION

In this chapter we have seen the powerful influence of the family to mold a young person's heart in good or bad directions. I am not saying that if a child develops unhealthy perfectionist traits it is all the parents' fault. Genes, temperament and the choices of the child obviously play a part too.

I noted earlier that there is a difference between the actual and perceived characteristics of demanding parents. Often it is a combination of both: highly sensitive children may perceive their parents to be far more demanding and critical than more laid-back and less sensitive children, but parents must do all that they can to minimize the dysfunctional, shaming aspects of their relationships, which often build unhealthy emotional habits in their children.[7]

In the next chapter we will look at how the culture of some countries breeds perfectionism, and we will also look, in more detail, at the influence and enormous power of the media, as it breeds discontent with our lifestyles, our families and ourselves.

QUESTIONS FOR DISCUSSION

1. Review the ways that parents can contribute to unhealthy perfectionism.

2. If a child has a genetic tendency toward perfectionism, how might the parents help this trait to remain in the healthy range of the spectrum of perfectionism?

3. How have you been influenced in positive and negative ways by your parents?

4. If you are a parent, do you have any unhealthy perfectionist tendencies that might be having destructive effects on your children?

10

THE PRESSURES OF
CULTURE AND MEDIA

Culture is traditionally defined as the customs, values, attitudes and beliefs shared by a group of people. On a large scale, we have national and ethnic cultures, and on a smaller scale, a multitude of subcultures, such as family, church, school, college or military. Then there are subcultures, and even global cultures, created by particular styles of music, the Internet, advertising and Hollywood (or Bollywood) movies. We will look briefly at a few perfectionist subcultures and national cultures. In the second half I will focus on the culture of perfectionism created by the visual media, especially in North America.

There are some subcultures, such as military or medical (especially high-tech surgery), where it is, understandably, very important to maintain standards of order, precision, excellence and cleanliness. These are two particular occupations where standards of performance (and appearance in the military) must, of necessity, be kept very high. But rigid conformity to particular dress codes and rituals in most other circumstances is usually unhealthy.

Consider an example of a college subculture in the United States. Sarah, a graduate student, told me how much she tried to please her parents and teachers by excelling academically in high school. When she began attending a conservative, southern university, she immediately felt the pressure to conform to the "campus-wide focus on female beauty": At first she was intimidated by the amount of time and attention the other girls gave to their appearance, but soon she, too, was sucked into the same subculture of "shopping, dressing and talking about the two." She wrote:

> The credit card bills grew higher and higher, but my confidence grew in equal proportion. By the beginning of my second year, I had become a "trendsetter," someone whose clothes were constantly out on loan and whose dorm room was always filled with girls asking for fashion advice. I found pride in knowing that I always looked the part. By my senior year I was more than a trendsetter, I was a fashion snob. I scoffed at labels like Gap and Banana Republic and owned more than 120 pairs of designer shoes. It is important to know that when I arrived on campus three years prior, I owned only 7 pairs of shoes!

Sarah felt great because she had succeeded in fitting in and becoming a leader in her college culture. She loved the attention she attracted at parties, wanting only "to be the best!" It would have been hard to resist feeling ashamed of herself if she had not had the money or the natural good looks to keep up with the "perfect" appearance.

NATIONAL AND ETHNIC CULTURE

I sometimes ask my students which cultures they think of as being more perfectionist. The most common answers are German and Japanese because of their particular attention to order, precision and detail, as well as their ability to produce superior cars and electronic equipment. Switzerland—renowned for its clean cities, the world's most accurate timepieces, and trains and buses that run exactly on time—is also a common answer.

Asian, African and Indian cultures. Many cultures in the world tend to be more family- and group-oriented than our more individualistic Western culture. Shame is a common experience when family and social expectations are not met. Open expressions of approval or affection from parents to children are rarely seen. We hear of suicides among young Japanese students who fail exams and fear the disapproval of their family. The research on perfectionism shows that Asian American parents are often perceived by their children as being more critical and demanding than Caucasian American parents. One study found that Asian American college students had higher levels of unhealthy perfectionism than Caucasian American college students.[1] Offending subcultural, family or group norms is very serious; disapproval or ostracism is greatly feared. Other studies have shown that Asian Americans tend to score higher on scales of perfectionism—both healthy perfectionism, which leads to high achievement, and unhealthy perfectionism, which may precede anxiety and depression.

Joseph, a student of mine, grew up under the influence of American and Chinese cultures. He wrote to me of his struggle with shame and fear of failure:

> In my mind, I could still hear my father sigh a long sigh and say: "You can't do anything right." The words haunted me during a significant event or even at times when I was relaxing at home. They came whispering through even though I had worked it through in my mind.

His father did not believe in recreation or relaxation and always scolded his children when he found them watching television or taking a nap. Typical of many immigrants with the pressure to survive and succeed, he worked twelve-hour days and didn't want his family to be unproductive. His mother, on the other hand, did not criticize her children, but neither did she give affirmation. She grew up in China and was taught that humility, especially in public, is a very important virtue. When someone complimented her, she would respectfully refuse their commendation. When people said good things about her son's behavior or performance, she would similarly deny the compliment. It was not polite to accept a compliment as if it was deserved, even when it was fully appropriate, for it might be misconstrued as being proud.

Even though Joseph knew that his parents cared about him, he never heard a word of affirmation, affection or encouragement from them. When it came to discipline and scolding, words and spankings flowed freely. In retrospect, Joseph feels that he was craving attention from his parents by trying to be perfect. He concluded:

> Everything that I do must be done right. If you do things right, you always succeed. If you don't succeed, you didn't do something right. So if there is a failure, something was not done perfectly. This standard has helped me to do my best, but it has also caused great grief and debilitation. It sets the bar so high that sometimes it cannot be reached. I am dogged by a fear of failure.

North American and European culture. Our Western culture has been described as guilt-based and individualistic in contrast to shame-based Asian cultures, which find their identity more in relation to family and social groups. As Western culture has moved away from its Christian foundations in the last three hundred years, Westerners have less reason to feel guilt in relation to God or any absolute standard, and values come to be defined more and more in relation to one's social or subcultural group. Character and moral values are far less important today than how much money we have or how we look. For many, their cultural heroes have become those whose faces and bodies appear in *People* magazine. Visual images are so powerful and pervasive that pressure for appearance perfectionism is everywhere. The "beautiful" people that we want to know about are the movie stars, supermodels, sports heroes and business billionaires. These are the "perfect" people whose lifestyles and looks are paraded before us for comparison with ours. People have always made comparisons, but we are bombarded in a unique way by exposure to TV, film, glossy magazines and computer images. We can see many beautiful people in one evening. The media shapes our expectations, desires and fantasies.

SEARCHING FOR THE PERFECT BODY

For young women entering puberty, with all the physical and hormonal changes, there is a critical conflict because many of the models in *Vogue*, *Teen* and *Shape*, in TV shows and movies, and in most of the advertisements and clothing catalogues are unusually thin. Irresponsible advertisements are aimed at adolescents, such as one in *Teen* for a secret weight-loss formula, with headlines such as "Get the perfect body you've always wanted" or "How I lost 37 pounds and had the best summer of my life. . . . Love life takes off. . . . Suddenly there are parties and dates and kisses and fun!" The message is the same: to be acceptable and liked by the boys, you have to look like the models in the fashion magazines with their fantastic bodies, flowing hair and flawless complexions. In reality it probably takes the models two hours to put on the makeup, which is paid for by someone else, and when the shooting is over, the air brush technicians get to work on the photographs to get them as close to perfection as possible. The average model is thinner than 95 percent of Americans. No wonder we have seen a huge increase in the incidence of eating disorders in recent years. No wonder the enormous amounts spent on plastic surgery grow each year.

A special report, "Searching for the Perfect Body," in *People* magazine demonstrated the driving power of the media to instill shame in vulnerable and insecure young women. In a telephone poll of one thousand women, the magazine found that "only 10 percent of respondents said they were completely satisfied with their bodies, and 80 percent said images of women on TV and in movies, fashion magazines and advertising made them feel insecure about their looks."[2]

Cosmetic surgery has been the subject of Oprah's shows and ABC's *Extreme Makeover.* The latter promises to give participants "a truly Cinderella-like experience by changing their looks completely in an effort to transform their lives and destinies, and to make their dreams come true."[3] In another television show on the same subject, *Nip/Tuck,* one of the main characters says to the doctor, "I don't want to be pretty. I want to be better. I want to be perfect. . . . When you stop striving for perfection, you might as well be dead." Nancy Franklin wisely commented that the "real undercurrent of the drama is the tyranny of appearances and the questionable morality of making a living by taking advantage of people's anxieties."[4]

Recent research has shown that "women who are surrounded by other attractive women, whether in the flesh, in films or in photographs, rate themselves as less satisfied with their attractiveness—and less desirable as a marriage partner."[5] I heard an example recently when a close friend's teenage daughter came home from a movie and bemoaned how bad she felt about herself as she watched Gwyneth Paltrow's perfect face on the big screen. In the television teen satire *Popular,* "Gwynethness" was highly valued, and an overweight girl was scorned as "eyesore candy."

A *New York Times* article by Alex Kuczynski, titled "Globe-Hop, but Beware Beauty Lag," describes the different standards of beauty in London, New York and Los Angeles. "London is definitely way laid-back," says Tara Reid, an actress who lives in Los Angeles but often visits New York and London. She says that manicures will reveal a woman's hometown as accurately as her driver's license: few manicures in London, a French manicure in New York and "in Los Angeles, you go totally, totally for color, and have red, super-red nails . . . and toes *must* match the hands. Whatever the season. Or else, just don't leave the house." Lucy Dahl, an English screenwriter, said, "In Los Angeles, there is a manicure salon every 10 feet, a plastic surgeon every 20 feet and a psychiatrist every 30 feet, which guarantees a life of perfect toes, perfect bodies and perfect mental health."[6] Below this article in the *New York Times* was a large Versace ad with near-naked male and female beauties on a beach. This inescapable visual environment influences us so that many of us feel ashamed if we do not measure up to the cultural standard of beauty and thus the standard of perfection for which we should strive. Perhaps one reason for the current epidemic of obesity is the sense of failure and defeat in those who are prone to the all-or-nothing thinking of perfectionism.

The effect on men. Men are deeply affected by the media too. In an article in *Psychology Today,* titled "Why I Hate Beauty," Michael Levine, the head of a public relations agency in L.A. and Hollywood, laments, "You might expect that [being around beautiful women] to make me feel good, as we normally like being around attractive people. But my exposure to extreme beauty is ruining my capacity to love the ordinarily beautiful women of the real world, women who are more likely to meet my needs for deep connection and partnership of the soul."[7] He describes research that demonstrates that, for men, "viewing pictures of attractive women weakens their commitment to their mates. Men rate themselves as being less in love with their partner after looking at *Playboy* centerfolds than they did before seeing the pictures of beautiful women." We are bombarded with similar images as we wait at the supermarket checkout, and "these images make us think there's a huge field of alternatives. It changes our estimate of the number of people who are available to us as potential mates. In changing our sense of the possibilities, it prods us to believe we could always do better, keeping us continually unsatisfied."[8]

Increasingly, television commercials are targeting men. There have been many comments about the impossible proportions of Barbie and other young women in cartoons, but now G.I. Joe and Luke Skywalker have been spending long hours in the gym! Harrison Pope, a Harvard psychiatrist, says that the original G.I. Joe scaled to human dimensions, would "have a bicep circumference of about 11 inches, similar to an ordinary man." G.I. Joe Extreme "(the most recent update in the list of action figures) would have a bicep circumference of 26 inches, larger than any body-builder in history."[9] Abercrombie & Fitch advertisements, and many men's health and fitness models, shame many average young men into obsessive body building and perhaps the use of steroids or other "muscle making" chemicals.

When young people have no foundation for identity, then they are extremely vulnerable to being brainwashed by the cultural norms of acceptance and images of perfection. In our media dominated culture, image becomes far more important than reality, and outward appearance more critical for success in life than inner character. Sadly, this is a terrible lie that is believed by many young people.

CHANGING STANDARDS OF BEAUTY

There is evidence that symmetry of facial features is valued throughout the world. Apart from that, standards of beauty and perfection change over time and between cultures. The search for perfection is deeply embedded in the human psyche. In her article "The Price of Perfection," Robin Marantz Henig helps us to keep perspective as she comments that, in the centuries-old "quest for beauty," women have done things to their own bodies or to the bodies of their children that sound horrifying. They have "mauled and manipulated just about every body part—lips, eyes, ears, waists, skulls, foreheads, feet—that did not quite fit into the cookie-cutter ideal of a particular era's fashion."[10]

In China, because people believed that small feet on an adult would be more beautiful and attractive to men, babies' feet were bound. In Africa, babies' heads have been wrapped to produce a cone shape that signifies beauty and intelligence. Hoops were inserted in lips and earlobes, and rings were used to stretch necks. In some parts of Africa, in contrast to our culture, obesity is a sign of prosperity and high social status. All sorts of devices have been used through the ages to shrink or enlarge waists, breasts and hips.

In the sixteenth century, many high society women, including Queen Elizabeth I, searching for unblemished facial skin, used a poisonous cocktail of vinegar and lead. The queen's face became so badly pitted that she had to cover it with layers of paint. Eventually she banned all mirrors from the royal court. In order to create blonde hair color, women at that time used powerful and damaging chemicals.[11]

Today, many are willing to go to amazing lengths to overcome dissatisfaction with their bodies as they pursue the image of perfection projected by the media in the hope that it will bring peace of mind.

Certainly it is good to care for our bodies, but pursuing health and developing inner character are far more likely to satisfy than energetically chasing external beauty and physical attractiveness.

In the next chapter I will move from external influences (family and culture) to internal psychology, exploring ideas about perfectionism that arise from the work of Freud and other psychoanalysts—where there are some intriguing connections to theology.

QUESTIONS FOR DISCUSSION

1. Have you ever belonged to a perfectionist subculture?

2. In what ways do you see other national/ethnic cultures as more or less perfectionist than your own?

3. How are you and, if you have them, your children affected by the "search for the perfect body"?

11

ANAL FIXATIONS AND OTHER
WEIRD AND WONDERFUL IDEAS

Early psychoanalysts spent many hours listening to people's experiences of childhood. While some of their theories are fanciful and misleading, there is much that rings true to our experience and gives helpful insight into the roots of perfectionism.

Freud believed that perfectionism and obsessive-compulsive tendencies are caused by what he called a "fixation" at the anal stage of life. Have you ever said about someone, "He's so anal"? The anal stage (eighteen months to three years) of development, when the parents are anxious that the child should be potty trained, comes after the oral stage with its preoccupation with food and exploring objects with the mouth. In the anal stage, children begin to realize that they have some control over when and where they empty their bowels.

Freud believed that the characteristics of the obsessive, retentive, miserly type of person were rooted in the child's ability to control his parents by holding everything in while on the pot. Freud was certainly right that there is a struggle in the child's mind in relation to his parents, but it has not so much to do with potty training itself as it has to do with issues of power and control. Often an eighteen-month-old begins to experiment with exerting his or her own will, along with showing signs of separation and independence, and the mother may respond with anger. The child may then have to deal with internal feelings of resentment or even hatred toward the mother. At the same time, the child will feel a tremendous need for the mother's comforting presence. There will be an oscillation between love and hate, submission and defiance, dependence and independence. I noted in chapter seven that these extremes are common in the adult perfectionist. In a good and loving home the child experiences patience, understanding, gentle but firm boundaries, and consequences, appropriate to their age, for disobedience. When these factors are present, the child learns to contain the extreme swings of emotion in a healthy way.[1]

Harry Stack Sullivan, a post-Freudian psychotherapist and analyst, believed that the roots of perfectionism lie in the insecurity and uncertainty of a family where there is confusion and chaos and little love.[2] Gary, a student, described his family as "feast or famine. It either was secure and warm, or it was chaotic, scary, and full of rage and emptiness. I would wake up each day not knowing which it was going to be. Therefore I controlled my own small world." His anxiety was especially severe when he was eight years old and his parents would quarrel loudly in the next room, often threatening divorce. He found that his only way to relieve his fear was to keep things in order in such a way that when he woke up to a world that was chaotic, he could then retreat to his own private world, which was ordered and secure. He concluded: "What I have carried away from my childhood (among other things) are two ongoing battles, one of loneliness and the other, an intense desire to control my environment and the people around me."

Leon Salzman, author of *Treatment of the Obsessive Personality,* believes that this obsessive defense is widely used "to achieve some security and certainty for the person who feels threatened and insecure in an uncertain world."[3] Salzman concluded that two passions are at the heart of the obsessive and strongly perfectionist personality: first, the hatred of being a limited person in an uncertain world, and second, a love for the illusion of control and the possibility of making life predictable. Feeling threatened, the perfectionist tries to feel in control by assuming that he or she is, or can be, omniscient and omnipotent. Control over oneself and one's environment is essential in order to avoid feeling helpless and powerless.

Alfred Adler—an analyst whose childhood physical deformity made him feel particularly inferior to others—believed that most of us suffer from feelings of inferiority stemming from our experience of powerlessness as young children and also from our inability to live up to an ideal of perfection.[4*] And Karen Horney noted that even at an early age we develop idealized images of ourselves to cope with feelings of insecurity, shame, inferiority and self-hatred,[5] but our inferiority is reinforced when we cannot live up to them. These psychoanalysts believed that issues of insecurity and inferiority were the roots of perfectionism.

Salzman sees obsessive-compulsive thoughts and behavior as a self-protective "device for preventing any feeling or thought that

---

*He saw that some people channeled their desire for perfection and power into socially useful avenues and were healthy, normal perfectionists who achieved a great deal in life. Others, neurotic in their perfectionism, became preoccupied with superiority and power. Thus, Adler, in the 1930s, saw the distinction that has reemerged in psychology in recent years between normal and neurotic perfectionism.

might produce shame, loss of pride or status, or a feeling of weakness or deficiency."[6] His diagnosis, which is purely psychological, is virtually identical with the biblical diagnosis of the central problem of human nature (although he does not express it in relation to God). We do not like being finite and limited. When things feel insecure and dangerous we try to take control of our world. Sometimes we try to control other people's worlds as well. The problem, at the heart of it all, is that we cannot trust that God is in control. In reaction, we develop what Dennis Gibson calls a "lust for omnipotence,"[7] the desire to be God.

Rachel, like many young people whose parents' marriages have fallen apart, struggles with "a strong desire for control and security." Her parents divorced when she was two years old. There was always tension between them, and she remembers longing for peace and stability. To compensate for the lack of security created by her parents' rivalry, she learned how to please these people who could cause pain and chaos. She achieved this by conforming her behavior to what she thought they desired or by manipulating situations to prevent confrontation. She told me,

> The ultimate issue is an attempt to control my world as much as possible in order to prevent painful experiences. . . . To some degree, I believe I can be my own god by manipulating my world in a way that brings fulfillment and joy in life independent of God. . . . But the truth is, in all my years, this ideal of controlling my world to avoid pain has never truly worked.

MEMORIES AND LONGINGS

I have been discussing the beginnings of life in relation to parents and families, but I want to move now into a new area of thought. There is a deeper reality behind, beyond and beneath what we see around us. It stretches back in time to our beginnings and reaches forward to our destiny. The most accepted belief in our scientific age is that we originated billions of years ago in the primal ooze and that time, chance and evolution have made us what we are today. In this view, there is no perfect beginning to which we look back, and there is ahead of us only an uncertain future, with the hope that we will evolve into more sophisticated and civilized creatures. In this evolutionary framework no end point of perfection exists; there is only an endless process of development. The biblical account of our origins is rather different. It gives clues to our aspirations for perfection in a way that the evolutionary model does not. It tells us that we were originally made perfect and placed in a perfect world.

The book of Genesis tells us that when God saw all that he had made, he pronounced it very good (Gen 1:31). The implication is that God's creation was perfect until it was marred by Adam and Eve's disobedience. If this account is really true, then it would not be surprising that we have a memory of, and longing for, that original perfection built into our psyche. The Bible also tells us that we are made for something more than we experience daily in our imperfect, fallen state, and that some day the original harmony and perfection of creation will be restored. So, not only do we have memories of a perfect past, we have the expectation and hope of fulfillment and perfection in the future. J. R. R. Tolkien wrote a letter to his son in which he reflected on this longing: "Certainly there was an Eden on this very unhappy earth. We all long for it, and we are constantly glimpsing it: our whole nature at its best and least corrupted, its gentlest and most humane, it is still soaked with the sense of 'exile.'"[8]

I am suggesting that many of our aspirations and longings reflect the reality of who we really are, flawed but destined for a restored and renewed creation. David Benner, a psychologist, writes in *Psychotherapy and the Spiritual Quest*:

> The quest for perfection is, therefore, a spiritual quest. It is the quest for wholeness. Much more than the quest for an absence of mistakes, it is the longing for the ideal, for that which is right, beautiful and pure. While it is easy to view such longings as naïve expressions of innocence, a person who has lost all idealism and drive for perfection is a person to be pitied. Perfectionistic longings continuously remind us of our failings and limitations, but without such reminders we would more easily forget the paradise which, while lost, is the place for which we long.[9]

In this chapter I have moved through some psychoanalytical ideas to larger philosophical and theological perspectives on perfectionism. The final section of the book will develop these further.

QUESTIONS FOR DISCUSSION

1. How does insecurity and inferiority predispose to perfectionism?

2. What do you think about the origin and destiny of human beings? Where did we come from? Where are we going? How do we know?

3. What do you think of the idea that we have a memory of, and longing for, perfection built into our psyche?

12

PERFECTIONISM AND PRIDE

The Road to Hell . . . or Heaven?

It is possible to deal with unhealthy perfectionism on a pragmatic level, using insights from psychologists and the practical ideas that I'll discuss in the next chapter, but in order to touch the deepest layers of the problem I need to delve further into theology and philosophy. As I mentioned in the introduction, our exploration of perfectionism will take us to the heart of Christianity. There have been hints of this along the way, especially in the last chapter, but in this and the following chapters, that is where we are going.

Up to this point, I have been talking about perfectionism as a hardwired genetic tendency, as a reaction to shaming and hypercritical parents, and as a response to the values of our culture. In the last chapter I revealed some of the deep roots of perfectionism in childhood insecurity and the resultant desire to be in control, and then I reflected on the built-in longing for perfection that may arise out of a memory of our origins and an anticipation of our destiny. Now I want to suggest that another root of perfectionism is pride.

PRIDE AND CONTROL

Pride. Although perfectionists seem very insecure, doubting their decisions and actions, fearing mistakes and rejection, and having low opinions of themselves, at the same time, they have excessively high personal standards and an exaggerated emphasis on precision, order and organization, which suggests an aspiration to be better than others.

Most psychological explanations see the desire to be superior and in control as compensation for feelings of weakness, inferiority and low self-esteem. But it could also be that the opposite is true; we feel bad about ourselves because we are not able to perform as well, or appear as good, as we really think we can. We believe we are better than others, but we keep discovering embarrassing flaws. Perfectionists' black-and-white thinking takes them on a roller coaster

CAUSES OF PERFECTION

Internal and External Influences

1. genes and temperament
2. culture
   - norms, models, heroes
   - advertising
3. family
   - modeling (example)
   - insecurity
   - demanding, critical and shaming parents
   - parental abuse or neglect
   - parental anxiety and overprotection
4. school or work (shame)
   - peer pressure
   - teacher/coach/boss
5. false church expectations and teaching
6. self-protection
   - fear of failure
   - fear of rejection
   - fear of loss of control
7. beliefs about the nature of reality
8. pride: the desire to be superior or the best

between feeling horribly inadequate and bad about themselves, and then, when things are going well, feeling proud to be so good. Low self-esteem and pride coexist in the same heart.[1] Psychologist Terry Cooper puts it well: "If I search around long enough, I'll find insecurity beneath my grandiosity and arrogant expectations beneath my self-contempt."[2]

Control. It is obvious that a desire to be in control is sometimes a protection against insecurity. But consider very young children who grow up in secure and loving families. Even there, one of the first words they learn is "no!" And, as adults, there is something in our hearts that resists being dependent on, and submissive to, anybody else. This reality is described in the biblical story of Adam and Eve. We are told they lived in a perfect world, in which there was no pain or difficulty. Satan—an angel who, in his pride and wanting to do things his way, had already rebelled—sowed doubt in their minds about the goodness of God, suggesting that God was keeping some knowledge and power from them, and tempting them with the lie that they could be like God: omnipotent, omniscient and in control (Gen 3:5). While some desire for control was legitimate, since God had given them "dominion" over creation—to care for it and develop its resources—rebelling against their finiteness and their Creator was going too far.

It seems that we, even more so with the insecurities and struggles of a fallen world, have a deep propensity to want to be in control. We do not like to accept that we are finite and limited, or that we might have to trust someone bigger than ourselves. I remember one young man, after battling for hours over questions about the origins of good and evil, shouted out, "I hate being finite." He wanted to understand everything. He wanted to be like God.

From a Christian view of the world, here is one of the deepest motives of perfectionism: the desire to be ruler of our own world and to make sure we are in control. Freud was so close to the truth when he said that the heart of all human problems was the Oedipus complex, a man's desire to get rid of his father, the authority in his life. Freud, of course, meant our biological, human father. The Bible defines the root problem as rebellion and hardness of heart toward our heavenly Father, God (Rom 1:21-25).

Author Dorothy L. Sayers focuses on the central aspect of pride as she writes:

> It is the sin of trying to be as God. It is the sin which proclaims that Man can produce out of his own wits and his own impulses and his own imagination the standards by which he lives: that Man is fitted to be his own judge. . . . The name under which Pride walks the world at this moment is the Perfectibility of Man . . . and its specialty is the making of blueprints for Utopia and establishing the Kingdom of Man on earth.[3]

"Making blueprints for utopia" and establishing their own kingdoms is perfectionists' specialty! God made us with the choice of whether to serve him or ourselves. As Bob Dylan used to sing, we cannot avoid serving somebody. Jesus' solemn and difficult teaching is that if we choose to serve ourselves, organizing life purely on our own terms, establishing our own kingdom, perhaps denying the existence of God altogether, then that is a choice that goes on forever, thus cutting ourselves off from all that we are intended to be.

Some years ago, after I had given a lecture on perfectionism, a man came up to me and gave me a version of the Lord's Prayer that I think he had written. He called it "The Perfectionist's Prayer."

> Their Father, who may be in Heaven,
> Holy be my name.

My kingdom come,
My will be done,
In earth as it should be in Heaven.
I'll get my own daily bread,
(I can't trust you to do it)
But I can't possibly forgive my sins
As there are too many of them,
And they are always bound to happen.
And I can't see why I should forgive other people
As they are always hurting me.
And anyway they never do anything right.
I'm quite capable of leading myself into evil
Thank you very much.
And if you had made a good job of this world
In the first place, I wouldn't have to
Endure all the temptation.
Mine be the kingdom,
The power and the glory,
Forever and ever,
Amen.

This expresses well the tension and ambivalence perfectionists experience in many areas—in trusting God, accepting forgiveness, being tolerant and forgiving toward others, and in letting go of ultimate control. They live in their own personal hell of dissatisfaction, anger, confusion, longing and disappointment.

RITUAL, RELIGION AND GRACE

You may be wondering why my focus is on Christianity alone. All the great religions of the world, except one, have developed rituals and duties that are designed to make us feel more secure in an uncertain, lonely and threatening world. But, whether it is Islam, Judaism, Buddhism, Hinduism or Confucianism (and even in some versions of Christianity), believers can never be sure that they have done enough to make themselves acceptable to "God."

Author Philip Yancey tells of a British conference on world religions, some years ago, where the participants were trying to decide if there was any belief that was unique to Christianity:

> They began eliminating possibilities. Incarnation? Other religions had different versions of gods appearing in human form. Resurrection? Again, other religions had accounts of return from death. The debate went on for some time until C. S. Lewis wandered into the room. "What's the rumpus about?" he asked, and heard in reply that his colleagues were discussing Christianity's unique contribution among world religions. Lewis responded, "Oh that's easy. It's grace."
>
> After some discussion, the conferees had to agree. The notion of God's love coming to us free of charge, no strings attached, seems to go against every instinct of humanity. The Buddhist eight-fold path, the Hindu doctrine of *karma*, the Jewish covenant, and Muslim code of law—each of these offers a way to earn approval. Only Christianity dares to make God's love unconditional.[4]

This is why Christianity has such a profound answer to some of the issues at the heart of perfectionism. The philosopher and theologian Francis Schaeffer never tired of saying that Christianity is both the easiest and the hardest religion. His reasoning was that it is the easiest because we do not have to do anything to contribute to our salvation; we need only come with empty hands and a repentant

heart to receive the free gift of God's forgiveness and love. It is the
hardest because we are proud, and we do not want to be indebted to
anyone, not even God. We want to do something to ensure our own
salvation. But the core of Christianity is about receiving God's free gift
of grace.

BE PERFECT

Now some might ask, "But didn't Jesus tell us to be perfect?" ("Be perfect . . . as your heavenly Father is perfect" [Mt 5:48].) How can we
avoid a command like that? In addressing this important question,
we need to understand the context of Jesus' words and, in doing so,
deal with two related issues. First, what is the biblical meaning of
perfection? Second, does the Bible teach that we should or can be
perfect in this life?

Complete. Some knowledge of the original languages will help as
I turn, first, to the Old Testament, where the Hebrew word for perfection is *tamim.* The root of this word means "to bring to completion." That which is brought to its intended goal, where nothing
more has to be done to complete it, is perfect. *Tamim* describes an up-
right person, someone living in a right relationship with God whose
life is patterned after the character of God, without moral blemish or
defect (Job 1:1, 8; 2:3; Ps 101:2).[5]

Growing into maturity. In strong continuity with the Old Testament idea of "bringing to completion," the New Testament concept
of perfection is found in the word *teleios*, meaning "design, end, goal
and purpose." Paul implies that the purpose of our existence, toward
which God is moving us, is maturity in our relationship with Christ.
In Colossians 1:28 Paul wants to "present everyone perfect *[teleios]* in
Christ." The same word is translated in Colossians 4:12 as "mature."
In Ephesians 4:13-14 Paul refers again to becoming "mature *[teleios]*,

attaining to the whole measure of the fullness of Christ." He contrasts this maturity with the immaturity and imperfection of being like "infants, tossed back and forth" by false teaching. The apostle James writes of the testing and trials that produce perseverance and work toward making us "mature and complete" (Jas 1:4). Like Paul, he contrasts this maturity with the immaturity of the "double-minded man" who is very unstable (Jas 1:8). Our calling is toward the perfection of maturity and holiness.

It is this word *teleios* that Jesus uses when he tells us to "be perfect" (Mt 5:48). The tense of the verb is future indicative, implying that *this is our goal; it is not something that is expected right now.* The wider context of Jesus' teaching is the contrast between the behavior of the believer and the unbeliever. The nonbeliever loves his friends, Jesus says, but the Christian is expected to do that *and* to love his enemies. It is important to strive to become better people, not just to be content with who we are or how we measure up to the standards of the culture around us. The primary goal of the Christian life is to become more like Christ in every area of our lives. This is in distinct contrast to the perfection of image, achievement and lifestyle that we have considered thus far.

The apostle Paul, attempting to follow Jesus' teaching, recognized that perfection was to be completed in the future, in heaven, as he wrote: "When perfection comes, the imperfect disappears" (1 Cor 13:10), and again, "Not that I have already . . . been made perfect, but I press on to take hold of that for which Christ Jesus took hold of me" (Phil 3:12). Believers have been saved from their own self-centeredness and are now in the process of being changed into what God intends them to be.

As we see the goal more clearly, we realize our enormous dependence on God for his help. There is no way we can reach this level of maturity (perfection) on our own, since there is no such thing as perfection this side of heaven. Thankfully, that is just where God wants us to begin—with the realization of our weakness and our need of his grace and strength. We live in an imperfect world, and in some matters we have to accept that for the moment. But there are other things that we can and should change. God has given us the Holy Spirit to help us "accept the things we cannot change, [have] courage to change the things we can, and the wisdom to know the difference."[6] This change is the subject of the next chapter.

QUESTIONS FOR DISCUSSION

1. Do you think that pride could be one of the roots of perfectionism, or does perfectionism always arise from insecurity?

2. What do you think of Terry Cooper's statement: "If I search around long enough, I'll find insecurity beneath my grandiosity and arrogant expectations beneath my self-contempt."

3. In what ways do you try to control your life and/or the lives of others?

4. How do you make "blueprints for Utopia" and try to establish your kingdom on earth?

5. Can you identify at all with the confusion of "The Perfectionist's Prayer"?

6. Do you think that all religions have essentially the same message?

7. In what way is Christianity different?

8. Jesus said that we should be perfect. What did he mean?

13

LEARNING TO LIVE WITH IMPERFECTION

Strategies for Change

At last we have reached the chapter you may have been waiting for. You see all the signs of unhealthy perfectionism in your family and friends and want to know how to help them change—of course, you yourself are perfect the way you are!*

You may realize now that not only can you not make yourself perfect but you also do not have to be perfect to be accepted by God. However, I'd still like to give some practical strategies to help change deep-rooted, perfectionist thought patterns. These strategies are like the framework of a house; they need a good theological and philo-

---

*You may like to take a test to see how perfectionist you are. There is an online test at <www.queendom.com> built on questions about real-life situations that you might encounter and how you would react to them. You have to pay a $4-5 fee, and you will receive a score of your general perfectionist drive and then how much is self-oriented, other-oriented and socially prescribed perfectionism. It also gives practical advice and tips for each form of perfectionism. This is not a highly accurate, validated test, but it is useful.

sophical foundation to survive for long. In later chapters we will return to that foundation. But for now, here are some practical ideas that can be used by anyone, whatever they believe about God or about human nature and identity. They can be used on one's own, with the help of family or friends, or in the context of counseling.

INSIGHT AND RESISTANCE

Our gut instinct tells us that "the truth will set us free," that if we could understand our perfectionist ways of thinking, we would automatically and easily be able to change. However, this is only a partial truth, because we usually need both insight *and* practical ideas about how to change.

> **PRACTICAL STEPS TO CONFRONTING REALITY**
> 1. evaluate the pros and cons of perfectionism
> 2. recognize all-or-nothing patterns
> 3. keep a journal
> 4. have small and specific goals

We also need experiences of making mistakes or lowering standards and still being accepted. For perfectionists, this is a problem because they are good at intellectual analysis and rationalization and often use these gifts to avoid stepping into unfamiliar territory. If they keep talking, no action is needed! Another problem is that perfectionists often think their view of reality is accurate, they cannot be persuaded that anything is wrong with it, and they believe everyone else is or should be doing things the way they think they ought to be done!

PRACTICAL STEPS: CONFRONTING REALITY

So the first task is to confront reality. Usually this is a gradual process, but sometimes a crisis occurs that brings about change in a dramatic way. For example, a friend of mine moved (because of her husband's job) to a country in Africa where sand blew in from the desert through every crack in a very imperfect house. Cockroaches and lizards were permanent residents, electrical equipment was old and often broken, and the concept of time was completely different (to arrive an hour late for a meeting was not considered rude). The problem was that she was a perfectionist, and back home she had kept a clean and ordered household and made a point of being punctual for all events. Now, surrounded by dirt, imperfection and chaos, she had to change or go home! This proved a quick cure for her perfectionism—what behavior therapists call "flooding." Here are some ordinary and practical ways of working at confronting reality a little at a time.

Evaluate the pros and cons of perfectionism. The first thing to do is to help yourself, or your perfectionist friend or client, evaluate the pros and cons of thinking and living under the pressures of perfectionism. Most perfectionists have never even stopped to think that there might be two sides to perfectionism—because they sincerely believe that there could not possibly be any disadvantages. Psychologist David Burns, in his helpful article "The Perfectionist's Script for Self-Defeat," asked one girl to reflect on both sides. When forced to confront reality, she managed to list only one advantage (it produced very good work most of the time) compared to six disadvantages—some of which were: perfectionism made her so tight and nervous she could not produce fine work or even adequate work at times; she was often unwilling to risk the mistakes necessary to come up with a creative piece of work; and it inhibited her from trying new things because she was so preoccupied with being "safe."[1]

When the advantages and disadvantages are carefully defined, it is usually easy to see that the costs outweigh the benefits. However,

perfectionists are convinced that their way of thinking protects them
from mediocrity and prevents mistakes. They do not see clearly the
negative consequences of self-criticism, dissatisfaction and vulnerability to depression.

Recognize all-or-nothing patterns. Second, all-or-nothing,
black-or-white thinking must gently be exposed as an unhelpful way
of dealing with reality. This usually has to be done by a friend or
counselor patiently reminding perfectionists of, or questioning them
to help them see, how extreme their evaluations of day-to-day situations are. David Burns asks perfectionists "to spend a day investi-
gating whether or not the world can be evaluated in a meaningful
way using all-or-nothing categories."[2] Of course, some moral issues
are black and white: it is clearly wrong to murder, commit adultery,
cheat or steal. But perfectionists tend to extend absolute judgments
to many other areas of life as well. Are the walls in this room completely clean or completely dirty, or are there just a few dirty marks?
Was that sermon superb or yet another example of the most boring
sermon ever preached, or were there some good things in it? This
exercise usually demonstrates the irrationality of such dichotomous
thinking.

The psychologist Albert Ellis, the father of rational emotive behavior therapy (REBT), attacked the irrational demands at the heart of
perfectionist goals, writing that

> excessive striving to be perfect will inevitably lead to disillu-
> sionment, heartache, and self-hatred. . . . As long as you merely
> *wish for*, but not *demand*, their achievement, you will (says
> REBT theory) feel frustrated, sorry, and disappointed but not
> depressed, anxious, or angry when you do not achieve them.

Escalating your *desire* for success and accomplishment to a demand, and especially to a *perfectionistic* demand, is quite another matter! Listen to this: "I *absolutely must*—or under all conditions at all times—*perfectly achieve* my goals!" Or else? Or else you will tend to conclude that you'll *never* get what you want. Or else you'll be *totally* unworthy of approval and love by significant others. Or else you will be in *continual danger* of harm and annihilation. Quite a series of "horrors" you have predicted—and helped bring on yourself.[3]

Ellis assists his clients to see the all-or-nothing language and concepts that they are using, and helps them change to more rational thought patterns. "The beliefs 'I would *like* to perform well and often to perform perfectly well' are rational and self-helping. . . . But the beliefs 'I *absolutely must* perform well and indeed *must* perform perfectly well' are often irrational and self-defeating."[4]

Such insights are very helpful, but new habits of thinking and feeling take a long time to become established in the brain and heart.

Keeping a journal. In relation to extreme self-critical judgments, it is valuable to keep a "habitual thoughts and feelings" journal. This exercise makes you aware of automatic thoughts, the old tapes, that pop into your mind when under pressure. A meal you cooked turns out badly, and you sink into the depths of despair, vowing never to cook again because you are so incompetent. You have a crisis with your two-year-old, and you feel like a hopeless parent. You lose a game of tennis and are depressed for the rest of the day. In all of these situations, our identity depends on being successful, and a failure erodes our identity, leaving us with the certainty of our worthlessness. Until we record the pattern, we often will not realize how frequently these situations occur and how extreme our reactions are each time. We do not need to be victims of our habitual ways of thinking and feeling, but we will have to work hard to resist them and begin to make some changes.

I strongly recommend a very helpful book by Martin Antony and Richard Swinson, *When Perfect Isn't Good Enough*. They give many more practical steps toward change than I have space for in this book. Here is an example from the journal of one of my clients, modeled on the suggestion of the book.[5] I asked her to identify an everyday situation in her life where she finds herself critical of her husband.

Date: *November 12*

Time: *4:30 p.m.*

Situation: *I go to put the dishes in the dishwasher and find that my husband has put the dishes on the wrong rack; in addition, he hasn't rinsed them very well.*

Emotions: *frustration and anger*

Perfectionist Thoughts:
- *Why can't he do it the way it* should *be done?*
- *The bowls* should always *go in the wider spaces, and the dishes* should *be thoroughly rinsed.*
- *Why can't he be systematic? Then there would be more space, and the dishes wouldn't get chipped.*
- *Why is he* always *so stubborn? Why does he* never *respect my opinions?*

Alternative Thoughts:
- *I believe my way is better, but there are other ways to load the dishwasher. A few crumbs probably don't make that much difference.*
- *He only loads the dishwasher part of the time, and I can always move things when I do it.*

- *I shouldn't let something like this ruin all the good in our relationship.*
- *I have to admit that he is not stubborn about most things.*

Conclusions:
- *This is a small matter in the wider scheme of things.*
- *I don't need to get so angry about it; my anger doesn't help the situation. In fact, it probably makes it worse because it irritates him and makes him more stubborn.*
- *Perhaps if I stop nagging him, he will be more likely to change.*
- *He does listen to me and respect my opinions in most things. It is unfair to say he never listens.*

This example demonstrates the movement from identifying habitual thought patterns, learning to question them and then beginning to experiment with new and more reasonable thoughts. This is the way a cognitive psychotherapist would help a client to retrain their thoughts and emotions.

At this point, if you are a perfectionist, you may have recognized some of the patterns. You may be excited about your wonderful new life and the great changes you will make—today! Do you see a pattern of all-or-nothing thinking? When I explain again that it will have to be little by little, you may get very discouraged and feel like giving up the struggle. It is very hard to learn to live between the extremes of all or nothing, but that is the most important task in learning to live with imperfection. In an article on helping religious adolescents with perfectionism, B. Sorotzkin observes, "This is more difficult than it sounds since it is very painful for someone with a poor self-image to give up the dream of glory inherent in perfection for the, as yet never experienced, joy of gradual emotional growth."[6]

PRACTICAL STEPS: MOVING FROM IDEALISM TO REALITY

Most perfectionists do not live in reality because they assume that setting the highest possible standards always leads to optimum performance. Somehow they need help to move from this *idealism* to *realism*. Some counselors suggest "aiming for average,"[7] but this is a nightmare for most perfectionists. With all-or-nothing thinking, "average" is despised. Reality is being content with less than perfection, even though you may aim high. When my students are writing six term papers it would be foolish for them to expect to get an A+ on all of them, as much as they might like to do so. Learning to be satisfied with a B+ or B on all of them might be better for their sanity and health than aiming to "go for gold" on all of them.

Day by day: small and specific goals. Developing a day-by-day, little-by-little plan is helpful because general goals are inadequate. Those who struggle with procrastination often need help being accountable for planning ahead and setting intermediate tasks; otherwise they will never get started. It is important to break down each general goal into more specific goals.

Here are a few of the examples in Antony and Swinson's book. One person's general goal was becoming more tolerant of others, which was broken into subsidiary tasks such as: "a) Stop caring how my housemate washes the dishes; b) Learn how to tolerate my spouse arriving home thirty minutes late without phoning; c) Allow my children to make a mess when playing, as long as they clean it up by the end of each day [depending on their age, of course]."[8] Those who are particularly critical of others need to recognize and resist their judgmental thoughts. It is not wrong to have reasonably high standards, and we can certainly put our point of views in a thoughtful manner that is not demanding, controlling or contemptuous. But we cannot impose our standards on everyone else when they choose to do things differently, unless we are in a legitimate role of responsibility where that is necessary.

If the general goal is to be less perfectionistic about my physical appearance, then I will "a) Take no more than thirty minutes getting ready in the morning; b) Be able to miss a workout in the gym; c) Be willing to gain five pounds without getting upset."[9] If my general goal is to become less detail-oriented, then I will: "a) Tell stories to other people without having to include every detail; b) Hand in papers that are no longer than they are supposed to be; c) Submit monthly reports without checking them over more than once."[10] Now you can take some area of your life where you would like to be less than perfect and describe how you are going to do it.

You may remember Alice, from chapter eight, who wrote of the many factors that contributed to her perfectionism and about her mother who stripped and waxed the wooden floors every week. Recently I received a letter from her in which she described the progress she was making. She has come to understand that she had been trying to earn God's acceptance by her own efforts to be a good person. It was an enormous relief for her to know that she could not and did not have to be perfect! As she absorbed the truths of Scripture, she gradually let go of her perfectionism in many areas. She wrote:

> My house is comfortably inhabited, at times quite messily, by me and my family. My desk, at one time an example of frustrated perfectionist defeat, now is cluttered, but functional, and easily organized when projects are completed. I have learned to give control of my schedule to God, for its intricacies cannot be engineered by me. Areas of sinful perfectionism persist . . . my demand for efficiency and my consequent tendency toward im-

patience if it does not occur . . . my difficulty admitting errors and my often-demanding behavior with my spouse.

Now she struggles to help her "highly perfectionist daughter," in whom she sees many of her own earlier tendencies to all-or-nothing reactions.

IMPLEMENTING PRACTICAL STEPS: NECESSARY INGREDIENTS

Courage to fail. Perfectionists have to learn to move out of their comfort zones in many areas and begin to take small risks that may involve failure. They need courage to be less than perfect. When I worked at the English branch of the L'Abri Fellowship (a study center and community), we often played a half an hour of volleyball at a tea break in the morning and afternoon. Students and staff would have hilarious and unprofessional games. One young woman stood on the sidelines, day after day, for several weeks, refusing to join in lest she make a mistake and be the butt of people's jokes. Her parents were both perfectionists, and she had inherited, learned and chosen their thinking patterns. She was an excellent schoolteacher but prone to anxiety, depression and difficulty in close relationships. After some weeks she trusted us more and responded to gentle cajoling by stepping out on the court. She turned out to be quite a good player and discovered that even though she did make mistakes, so did everybody else, and it really did not matter! After that there was no stopping her. She played at every opportunity. Some months after she had returned to the United States, she wrote back to say that playing volleyball was probably more important, or at least as important, as the lectures, discussions, prayer and counseling she had been involved in while with us. "Now," she said, "I am taking risks in other areas of life as well. The lessons I learned in volleyball have generalized into the rest of my world." She was able to "see" emotionally that a mistake was not a total failure.

Openness to counseling. I have said already that there are particular difficulties for the therapist and a perfectionist client in counseling.[11] Specifically, it is hard for unhealthy perfectionists to trust other people, so it may be difficult to make the necessary therapeutic alliance, or good relationship, that is important for progress in therapy. Some perfectionists are resistant to any attempts to help them change; they may go along with the process in an attempt to please, while inwardly they may be ambivalent, anxious and angry. Others may fall into the trap of expecting the therapist to be perfect or of wanting to be the perfect client, constantly comparing themselves with other, real or imagined, "perfect" clients.

Perfectionists are caught in the contradiction of knowing, at one level, that they need help and, at another level, deeply resenting any suggestion that they are not perfect. Defenses and justifications are readily available, and these are preferable to admitting inadequacy, which can trigger despair. Perfectionists are stuck in ambivalence and all-or-nothing thinking about dependence and independence. They believe that the doctor, therapist or friend should be able to fix the problem for them and, at the same time, that they should be able to fix it on their own. The idea of a cooperative, mutual, helping relationship is difficult to accept.

What perfectionists really want from the counselor or therapist is to be made perfect and invulnerable, but the counselor is in the difficult position of regularly helping the clients to see the failures of their pattern of thinking and their inability to escape imperfection. Salzman puts it well:

When he (the perfectionist) discovers that, instead of making him a superman, therapy attempts to strengthen his humanness and get him to accept his imperfections, he is both angry and disappointed. Instead of an anxiety-free existence in a state of perfect living, he discovers that therapy will only help him to live with anxiety in an imperfect world in which he will have no ultimate control over his destiny. Such goals are so alien to him that he considers himself a failure for even approaching them. . . . As he becomes emotionally and psychologically more mature, he seems to feel that he is getting worse.[12]

Optimal environment for change. Individual counseling and friendships are very important, but there is a need for a wider context to facilitate change. It is very difficult to change old habits of thinking and feeling alone, or even with a counselor. We need a variety of other caring relationships. Ideally, in the family is where we first learn about love, acceptance and grace in the midst of failures. I realized how important this was for me when my father died a few years ago. As family and friends shared stories about him after the funeral, we laughed and cried together, and I pushed those who had worked with him to tell me more about their experiences of working with him in the hospital or family practice, of sailing and playing tennis with him. As I listened to how they described him, I became even more thankful for being raised in an environment where there were expectations, and discipline of course, but where there was always a deep knowledge of being loved and accepted, even in failure and foolishness. I found he treated everyone that way.

Sadly, so many know only a poisonous environment of the opposite of love and grace—what we might call un-grace or dis-grace. Thankfully those who have grown up with damaging relationships in their family can experience substantial healing in other more loving and grace-filled relationships (this may be in marriage, with extended family, friends or other groups).

The New Testament describes the church as a community, an alternative family. Ideally, we should experience acceptance and love there, renewing our thinking and feeling patterns, and strengthening the ability to resist the pressures of the world around us. We should be able to find friends who will gently challenge and humor us in our all-or-nothing thinking or unrealistic standards. Churches that model God's grace and forgiveness are places to be treasured.

Unfortunately, many churches give the impression that their first priorities are performance and appearance. The man who is struggling with addiction to alcohol or pornography, or the woman who is struggling with a difficult marriage or anorexia may take one look at an immaculate church building full of well-dressed, secure, smiling people and think that this is no place for them. If only this visitor could see beneath the surface and realize how good people are at covering up the mess of their faults and failures. However, there *are* churches and fellowship groups where one can observe honest and open confessions of life's struggles in a context of grace and acceptance.

Churches can also help heal our assumptions about God's character, which may have been affected by our experience of our parents, especially fathers. For example, Jim's father was unpredictable and controlling, prone to rages when his children did not obey instantly and without question. When Jim was moving toward faith in Christ, he struggled to separate his own image of fatherhood from God as a loving, patient and forgiving father. Even after he became a Christian, he found himself responding to God more out of terror of rejection or anxiety to please than out of thankfulness for God's love and acceptance. Gradually, as he learned more about God and experienced the acceptance of other men in his life, he began to respond to God in a different way from his father.

CONCLUSION

In our imperfection and immaturity we live with many conflicting voices about our desires, priorities and goals. We are drawn by the seductive sirens of cultural perfectionism. We are haunted by the voices of parental criticism, by our own self-critical thoughts, and by the devil's confusing and deceptive whispers. The latter is, after all, described as the "father of lies" (Jn 8:44). But God's Spirit is at work in us, and listening for his voice is vital for our health and sanity. It is often in the quietness of God's presence that we are able to hold the balance and stay in reality. That is why being still in the presence of God, praying, and studying and meditating on Scripture are vital in order to discern what is true and what is important. C. S. Lewis writes,

> the real problem of the Christian life comes where people do not usually look for it. It comes the very moment you wake up each morning. All your wishes and hopes for the day rush at you like wild animals. And the first job each morning consists simply in shoving them all back; in listening to that other voice, taking that other point of view, letting that other larger, stronger, quieter life come flowing in. And so on, all day. Standing back from all your natural fussings and frettings; coming in out of the wind.[13]

In this chapter, we have looked at practical strategies for helping the perfectionist accept and deal with imperfection. While these strategies are useful, to be effective and lasting they need a firm foundation beneath them. When someone begins loosening the grip of unhealthy perfectionism they must have a strong and reliable sense of identity and purpose, built on a foundation of reality and truth, that will allow them to grow toward a healthy pursuit of excellence. That foundation is the topic of the next chapter: who am I and what am I intended to become?

QUESTIONS FOR DISCUSSION

1. What are the pros and cons of perfectionism in your life and in the lives of family and friends?

2. In what ways do all-or-nothing patterns show themselves in your thinking?

3. What are your goals for change? How will you break down the general goals into realistic, specific, day-by-day goals?

4. Have you taken risks in being willing to fail or make mistakes recently?

5. Where in your life do or will you find the optimum environment that will help you change toward healthy perfectionism? Do you have friends or a group who are willing to help you?

6. How is your understanding of the character of God affected by your perfectionism?

THE SEARCH FOR
IDENTITY AND PURPOSE

Who am I? Who am I supposed to be? What would a perfect me be like? Do my job, my qualifications, my race, my clothes, my social status give me a sense of who I am—an identity? All of these things are certainly parts of our identity. A big question is whether there is anything substantial behind our appearance and performance, a core of personality and identity that is a given—something that may be molded and shaped by my environment but is essentially consistent throughout life? And is that core of who we are supposed to stay the same, or should it change and mature in some way throughout life? What is our purpose, our destiny? I hope that by the end of this chapter you will see how important these questions are in relation to perfectionism.

A QUESTION OF IDENTITY

There are many influences from people in our culture—parents, peers, fashion experts, ethicists, philosophers—telling us who we are and what we should be. These influences have existed, to one degree or another, in every culture, but until approximately three hundred years ago, in Europe and America, Christianity had been the most powerful influence for nearly two millennia in shaping ideas about human nature. People saw themselves as "made in God's image" and as having a unique significance and identity in the eyes of their Creator, which transcended the influence of parents, peers, philosophers and fashion. Since that time, in Western society, a majority has decided that there is no God—at least not the Judeo-Christian God who people used to believe in—so they are left to find a new source of identity. A 1999 issue of *The New York Times Magazine* was devoted to the theme of "The Me Millennium." On the cover was the sentence "We put the self at the center of the universe, now, for better or worse, we are on our own."[1]

Modernism and postmodernism. I live at the confluence of two great American rivers—the Missouri and the Mississippi. It is an impressive sight, and these rivers have had a huge influence on the development of the thousands of miles of land through which they run—sometimes very beneficial, sometimes profoundly destructive. In our culture, we live at the confluence of two highly influential rivers of thought: modernism and postmodernism.

These are the humanist and existential ideas that, over the last three hundred years, have replaced Christianity as the dominant worldview in our culture. They flow through and around us, affecting everything, often without being named or recognized, shaping both our way of thinking about ourselves and the world we live in— for good or ill.

Put very briefly, modernism is the belief that with science, reason and technology we can make our world a better place. Our identity, from the modernist perspective, is defined by the objective, scientific experts of genetics, anthropology, psychology, sociology, biology and other sciences. Reality is what can be described and measured. Biologists or sociologists, for example, tend to reduce the fundamentals of human nature to biological or sociological processes, respectively. God is no longer needed (in this modernist perspective) as part of the explanation of how things work or to give a moral framework for living.

However, even from the beginning of modernism, in what we call the Enlightenment, there was a reaction against this emerging mechanistic view of human nature. In an attempt to preserve the significance and dignity of persons in a scientific age, these reactionary movements—seen in romanticism, existentialism and mysticism—emphasized personal and subjective values almost to the exclusion of the mechanistic and objective. The pendulum swung to the other extreme. It was these ideas that became what we now call postmodernism, in which, without a reference point outside ourselves in revelation, reason or science, we are left only with subjective experience and freedom to choose to be whatever we want to be—to invent ourselves. Self-fulfillment becomes a core value.

Postmodernism, the contemporary expression of that reaction to modernism, now tells us that we have no core, "given" identity. There is no real, substantial *me*—no essential self. We are whomever and whatever we choose to be. For example, one place that we can experiment with this is on the Internet. In a chat room or while blogging, if we choose to do so, we can take on any identity that we wish because we cannot be seen. We can be a man or a woman, age eight or fifty, artist or doctor—and no one will know. In that virtual reality we can live without bodies. We can create any identity we choose. We can "appear" much better than we really are. In the "virtual reality" of computer games we can experiment with different personalities and behaviors. In the real, physical world it is not so easy to change our identity, but for some with enough money there is the possibility of transforming their appearance with plastic surgery, new, stylish clothes, another partner, a different car or, perhaps, an apartment in a trendy part of town. These are, of course, mostly external aspects of identity, but our culture tells us they are important. The inner subjective world of thoughts and feelings is much harder to change. The most extreme ideas of postmodern academia are not easy to live out in the real world.

If there is no essential self, if my identity is fluid, then I am judged only by my appearance, because that is all there is. Where there is no substance, we are left only with image enhancement and, as we saw especially for the appearance perfectionist, "impression management." As Lewis Lapham, editor of *Harper's Magazine,* wrote in an article about the loss of values and sense of self in our culture, "The loss of identity is good for business. . . . If I knew who I was, why would I keep buying new brands of aftershave lotion?"[2] Gertrude Himmelfarb, a history professor, describes in *The American Scholar* the loss of objectivity, truth and reality in postmodernism:

> Nothing is fixed, nothing is permanent, nothing is transcendent. Everything is in a state of total relativity and perennial flux. There is no correspondence between language and reality; indeed there is no "essential" reality. What appears to be true is nothing more than what the power structure, the "hegemonic" authority in society, deems to be true.
>
> To those who have been happily spared this latest intellectual fashion, it may seem bizarre and improbable. I can only assure you that it is all too prevalent in all fields of the humanities. . . .
>
> Those who do not think of themselves as postmodernists often share the extreme relativism and subjectivism that now per-

vade the humanities as a whole. In the leading professional
journals today, the words *truth, objectivity, reason* and *reality*
generally appear with quotation marks around them, suggesting how specious these concepts are. What we are now confronting, therefore is not one revolution, but two—a
technological revolution and an intellectual revolution, which
bear an uncanny resemblance to each other and have a symbi-
otic relationship to each other. If I were given to conspiratorial
theories, I might speculate that Bill Gates, the chairman of Mi-
crosoft, is a secret agent of Jacques Derrida, the high priest of
postmodernism.[3]

Ironically, it is the technology of the modernist, scientific approach
(that postmodernists originally reacted against) that gives today's
postmodernists the power to mold and reshape themselves geneti-
cally, biochemically, cosmetically and psychologically to be whatever
they want to be. The amazing wizardry of twenty-first-century technology is used to surround us with images of "perfect" people in magazines and movies, to make it possible to alter our shape and appearance through cosmetic surgery, to enhance our performance by drugs
or genetic manipulation, and to create seductive advertisements of
perfect houses, gardens and vacation islands where we can live out
our fantasies. But, of course, much of this is only available to the few
who have the money to pay the price! The rest of us are left to dream!

A GIVEN IDENTITY

If we have come by chance from the primal ooze after millions of
years of evolution, then we can only define ourselves or let society or
the experts define us. But if there is a personal God who created us,
then the heart of the issue is not what others, or even we, think of

who we are. What really matters is what God thinks of us. We have a given or derived identity—not an identity that we create for ourselves. Society does not define me, I do not define myself; God defines me. I cannot merely say with some philosophers, "I think therefore I am" or "I feel therefore I am," or even "I am what I do" or "I am how I look." I can only say with accuracy that "I am who God has made me to be." If God exists, then an accurate understanding of what he thinks of me is vital to my health and sanity. The Bible tells us several foundational things about who we are and what we are becoming, about our identity and purpose.

Dignity. First, God sees us as people with great dignity. We are created "in his image," with the ability and capacity to love, think, feel, choose, create and have personal relationships just as he does. We are not just advanced animals or complicated machines. In the creation story, God delighted in all he had made. He gave Adam and Eve the responsibility of caring for creation. God greatly values the animals and birds, but human beings are the pinnacle of his creation (Mt 6:26; 12:12), the only created entity stamped with the Creator's image and "crowned with glory and honor" (Ps 8:4-8). Even Charles Darwin recognized something amazing about human beings when compared to monkeys, referring to man as "the wonder and glory of the universe."[4]

Reflected glory. The Bible speaks of our unique dignity, being made in the image of God, in another, less familiar way: the concept of glory. Jesus said that he had given his disciples the glory that God had given him (Jn 17:22). Paul put it slightly differently when he said that we all reflect God's glory (2 Cor 3:18). This is hard to grasp because we usually reserve the word *glory* for such events as a beautiful sunset or when an Olympic gold medal winner stands on the podium. In the Bible, the glory of God is seen in a few instances of dramatic light and color but mostly in his creativity and character.

Adam and Eve reflected God's creativity, and hence his glory, as they named the animals. They and their descendants were the first scientists, exploring the world, categorizing creation, making new discoveries, gardening and farming. Today part of humanness and reflected glory is our ability to develop the resources of creation, to cure diseases and explore space. It is also seen in the beauty and creativity of musical, artistic or athletic ability. Eric Lidell, one of the runners portrayed in the film *Chariots of Fire,* realized that God had given him an extraordinary gift that he could not neglect. It was part of his created glory as a human being. As he disciplined himself to develop this ability, he said, "When I run, I feel God's pleasure."[5] To see other people doing what God made them to do, whether making music, playing sports, caring for children, analyzing a math problem, doing carpentry, cooking a good meal or listening well to those in trouble, is to see them expressing something of their God-given glory. This is what it means to be truly human.[6]

This forces me to examine how I see the people around me. How, for example, do I view my wife? Too often I take her for granted and, because of my own self-centeredness, notice her defects and shortcomings rather than her gifts and dignity. Authors Dan Allender and Tremper Longman write: "To view our spouses from the lens of glory is to be overwhelmed by the privilege of being face to face with a creature who mirrors God."[7] As I have seen the development of my wife's gifts of loving our children, caring for people, hospitality and floral design, it has been like watching a beautiful flower opening toward its full glory.

Depravity. The other side of the picture of human beings is that, since the Fall, we are creatures of great depravity and perversity, capable of the most horrific cruelty. Few people would doubt this after the pictures and stories from September 11, 2001, or from Rwanda, Kosovo, Afghanistan, Iraq and Sudan in recent years. This is not what God intended; it is a distortion of our humanity. Depravity is witnessed not only on a global scale but also on the local news, as we receive daily stories of sexual abuse and murder. The last century saw the worst examples of man's inhumanity in all of recorded history. This depravity is not new, however. It has been here since soon after human beings were created, when Adam and Eve chose to disobey God. The effects spread rapidly, as evidenced by the envy, bitterness, hatred and murder that appeared in the next generation (Gen 4:1-8); soon all human beings were deeply corrupt (Gen 6:11-12). We are indeed a strange, wonderful and terrible mixture of dignity and depravity, beauty and brokenness, glory and grief. John Stott put it well:

> I am a Jekyll and Hyde, a mixed-up kid, having both dignity, because I was created in God's image, and depravity, because I am fallen and rebellious. I am both noble and ignoble, beautiful and ugly, good and bad, upright and twisted, image of God and slave of the Devil. . . . We must be fearless in affirming all that we are by creation and ruthless in disowning all that we are by the Fall.

Here then is the paradox of our humanness. We are capable both of loftiest nobility and of the basest cruelty. One moment we can behave like God, in whose image we are made, and next like the beasts from whom we were meant to be distinct. Human beings are the inventors of hospitals for the care of the sick, universities for the acquisition of wisdom, parliaments for the rule of the people and churches for the worship of God. But they are also the inventors of torture chambers, concentration camps and nuclear arsenals. Strange, bewildering paradox—

noble and ignoble, rational and irrational, moral and immoral, godlike and bestial![8]

Ruined glory. Another way of seeing our depravity is as a deface-ment of our glory as human beings. The biblical account tells how our glory was originally spoiled by Adam and Eve's folly in disobeying God. Francis Schaeffer put it well when he described us as glorious ruins. Imagine a beautiful old palace or castle, built many centuries ago. You wander around the crumbling ruin with its high windows and old fireplaces and imagine the lords and ladies in their fine clothes in the banqueting hall before a roaring fire. You have a sense of its pre-vious glory and the tragedy of its destruction. You can also imagine what it would be like if it were to be completely restored.

Accepting that we are glorious ruins, with great dignity and pro-found depravity, is part of the tension of living in a fallen world. This ambiguity is hard for perfectionists to accept. They want to think that it is possible for life to be all glory, but one flaw or failure confirms the diagnosis of complete ruin. For them, the dignity and depravity are not woven together but are in two separate compartments. They are in either one or the other but find it hard to live in the tension of both at the same time.

THE CONTEXT OF FAMILY AND COMMUNITY

We have seen that our identity is primarily rooted in what God thinks of us, not what others think. But God made us to live in human rela-tionships, which do have a significant effect on what we think of our-selves. Postmodernism tells us that historical and social context are ir-relevant to a strong sense of identity, but in reality it is in contextual relationships of family and community, rooted in history, that we learn, ideally, about trust, love and grace. It is there that we are helped to have an accurate view of ourselves as a mixture of dignity and depravity. In the context of family I should learn not to think too much or too little of myself and that my fundamental worth cannot be changed by beauty, bucks, brawn, brains or BMWs—or lack of them.

Not only family but the wider community of extended family, friends and church (God's family) have a profound impact on shaping our sense of who we are, for good or ill, helping us to recognize our gifts and abilities, and our weaknesses and sins (Col 3:12-14; 1 Cor 12:14-27). Sadly, as I have shown in earlier chapters, family and others can also deeply damage our sense of identity when there is abuse, betrayal of trust, and lack of grace and love.

RESTORED GLORY

God is not a hypercritical, abusive or shaming father. Even though we are thoroughly mixed up and often rebellious, thankfully he doesn't give up on us. He is not an all-or-nothing thinker in the way he treats us; he accepts us in our imperfection. As I have shown, perfectionists have a hard time accepting grace. They give themselves, and sometimes others, little grace, so they do not expect it from God. In fact, the Bible tells us that he delights in us (Zeph 3:17), even though we are not perfect! He loves and values us so much that he welcomes us back into relationship and has begun to heal the devastating effects of sin.

Our value is reflected in the high price that he was willing to pay to redeem us and adopt us into his family (Jn 3:16; Rom 5:6-8; 1 Pet 2:9-10). Even though we fail him again and again, when we come to him in weakness and need, he offers grace, forgiveness and help in our ongoing struggles in life. God is determined that we should become all that he intended us to be—a "new creation" (2 Cor 5:17). God sees our potential and, in a sense, views us as having achieved that already. He accepts us for who we are and for what we will one day become, and not, as the perfectionist often thinks, because of what we do or how we look now. One day our true identity will be fully and completely revealed when we are unhindered by the flaws of this imperfect, broken world.

To put this in other words, our glory is being restored. In Old Testament Hebrew, the word *glory* carries the connotation of weight and heaviness. C. S. Lewis, in *The Great Divorce,* uses this meaning to describe the people who are heading away from God, living for themselves. They have become ghosts in that they are light, transparent, less real and less human. In contrast, the people who are heading toward God have increasing substance and weight. They become more substantial and less transparent in that they are more real and human.[9] God's intention is that we, the people of God, should become more like Christ, thus more substantial in our humanness. The full expression of our dignity and glory is seen as we become more fully what God intends us to be. This is the perfection toward which we are called.

God is in the business of refining us, and the prime place where that happens is in the context of relationships. Through suffering and difficulty he exposes our self-centered hearts and begins the process of inner transformation. "We," says Paul, "who . . . reflect the Lord's glory, are being transformed into his likeness with ever-increasing glory [from one degree of glory to another]" (2 Cor 3:18). It often does not feel like we are being changed, but little by little we grow in character and creativity, toward our full humanness.

When overwhelmed in day-to-day life with how frustratingly imperfect everything and everyone else is, and if I am honest, how imperfect I am, I need to be reminded of what I, and those around me, are becoming. A glimpse of their glory helps me to treat them with patience and dignity, and kindles hope and anticipation of one day being free.

The author Joseph Aldrich, writing about this transformation, sees intimations of a deeper reality in the stories we all read to our children:

> What do Cinderella, princesses kissing frogs, and ugly duck- lings have in common? All three describe a pilgrimage to beauty. Why does the delightful story of Cinderella endear itself to the hearts of millions of people around the world? Because one persistent prince is able to transform a lowly, unkempt, awkward servant girl into a charming, beautiful, graceful prin- cess. Whether it be princesses kissing frogs, ugly ducklings be- coming swans, or abused Cinderellas becoming belles of the ball, beauty is always irresistible.[10]

These stories have such a powerful appeal because they reflect the reality that we are all like frogs, ugly ducklings and abused servants, disfigured by our own and others' sin, awaiting the Prince to rescue us and set us free to be who we really are, for our true dignity and glory to be revealed.

REVEALED GLORY

Just as looking forward to a good vacation keeps me going in the dif- ficulties of day-to-day life so, in the bigger picture, we remember with Paul that "our present sufferings are not worth comparing with the glory that will be revealed in us." The whole creation, including us, he says, is groaning for the day when it will be liberated from its "bondage to decay" and imperfection. For now we wait eagerly for "the glorious freedom of the children of God" (Rom 8:18-25). When Christ returns, we will not have to struggle with the imperfections of a fallen world anymore. The creation will be renewed and restored. Our old nature will be completely gone, so we will no longer have to deal with pride, self-centeredness or the desire to be in control. We will, for sure, still be finite creatures of our Creator, but we will be able to accept this limitation without rebellion and fighting.

C. S. Lewis says it well:

> The command Be ye perfect is not idealistic gas. Nor is it a command to do the impossible. He is going to make us into creatures that can obey that command. . . . He will make the feeblest and filthiest of us into a god or goddess, a dazzling, radiant, immortal creature, pulsating all through with such energy and joy and wisdom and love as we cannot now imagine, a bright stainless mirror which reflects back to God perfectly (though, of course, on a smaller scale) His own boundless power and delight and goodness. The process will be long and in parts very painful; but that is what we are in for. Nothing less. He meant what He said.[11]

It may be difficult for perfectionists to hear that there is no shortcut to perfection. They want the change completed immediately or not at all. And the fact that it is painful—painful because sin is deeply embedded and the process of God teaching us is slow—is hard to endure. But he will never let us go. We can rest in that deep security and know that we have significance in being made in his image and in being a child of God, saved by his grace, not by anything we have done or earned. At the deepest level, understanding and experiencing God's grace is the key to unlocking the prison of perfectionism.

There are many mysteries about the "new heaven and . . . new earth" (Rev 21:1), but there are enough hints in Scripture to persuade me that what is coming will not be brand new. Rather, there will be a renewal and fulfillment of what has already been created with all the impurities of fallenness and sin removed. There will be integration, harmony, order, creativity, playfulness, beauty and love more wonderful than our wildest imaginings. We and the whole creation will be perfected, and God "will wipe every tear" from our eyes. No more frustration, depression, worry, insecurity or fear of failure and rejection; death, mourning, crying and pain will be gone, "for the old order of things" will have "passed away" (Rev 21:4). God himself will live among us, and we will be seen in all our God-given glory. Our focus will no longer be on our imperfections, insecurities and struggles; instead, we will focus on the glory of God and enjoy the restoration of all things in our work, play and relationships.

CONCLUSION

Early in this chapter I explored some of the secular and Christian influences that shape our identity and sense of purpose. Knowing who we are and who we are intended to be helps us to resist the cultural pressures to find our deepest identity in the images and ideals of perfection that we see all around us. Paul writes: "Don't let the world around you squeeze you into its own mold, but let God re-mold your minds from within" (Rom 12:2).[12] As the Spirit of God renews our thinking patterns we begin to recognize two lies: first, that we have to be perfect to be accepted, and second, that we will be judged and evaluated by God in the way that our culture assesses value—primarily on the basis of our performance or appearance.

I have tried to display a glimpse of our future perfection, and in the final chapter I will draw together the threads to help us live until that day with more patience, grace and wisdom. Building on this foundation of God-given identity and value, and a vision of our restoring glory, how can we resist the seductive sirens of perfectionism with their different definition of glory? And how can we pursue excellence and true perfection without falling into the traps of unhealthy perfectionism?

QUESTIONS FOR DISCUSSION

1. What are the influences that have shaped your sense of identity?

2. How has that sense of identity been influenced by modernism and postmodernism?

3. What is the Christian understanding of the source of our identity?

4. Who and what does the Bible say we are?

5. What does the Bible say about our purpose in this world?

6. What does it mean for you that you have great dignity and reflect God's glory?

7. Think of some ways in which that glory is marred or ruined.

8. How do you relate to the idea that you are someone who is depraved?

9. In what ways is your glory being recognized and restored?

10. What is your understanding of grace?

15

TOWARD MATURITY

The Healthy Pursuit of Excellence and Perfection

I have examined perfectionism and ideas about perfection from many angles, and it's time to draw things to a close. I have explored how images of perfection in advertisements, movies and fashion magazines affect our thinking, causing us to desire perfect bodies, clothes, skin, hair. We know that the glamorous and glossy, computer-enhanced and air-brushed images are not real, but often we are lulled into a stupor as the seductive sirens manipulate our senses, emotions and ability to reason. We begin to believe the lie. We are also led to believe that setting very high standards and giving enormous amounts of time and energy to achieve them is the high road to prosperity and happiness. This is felt acutely in North American culture. Many parts of the world live with great poverty and imperfection and know nothing of the prosperity that spawns these seductions. Although, as we have seen, there were images of "perfection" in previous generations, the effects were never so powerful without the technology and marketing tools of TV, film, commercials, glossy magazines and the Internet.

We cannot avoid tension and conflict, because God calls us toward beauty, perfection and glory—but his description of these is different from the definition of perfection that presses itself on our senses each day. The major themes of appearance and performance deserve one last look so that we can find a way to live in this difficult tension.

APPEARANCE

If you haven't seen the real thing, you probably have seen pictures of Michelangelo's statue of David in Florence. We have similar images of manhood, though far more mundane, in Olympic swimmers and gymnasts, Abercrombie & Fitch advertisements or, more extremely, in bodybuilders and professional wrestlers. One art critic wrote,

> Michelangelo's *David* . . . is a strapping specimen of early manhood at the peak of physical power and grace, superbly muscled and superbly spirited, filled with righteous anger and emanating intractable will and awesome force. . . . With the head of a beautiful Apollo and the body of a young Hercules, he is an apotheosis of all the most heroic qualities in all young heroes, a figure human in form but superhuman in his perfection of mind, body and soul. This *David* . . . is a portrait of an Ideal for which the Biblical David was simply a convenient symbol. This *David* is not Hebraic but Greek, not scriptural but Platonic.[1]

Michelangelo was influenced by Greek idealism and Neoplatonic thinking—the belief that things in the visible world, such as trees or people, represent imperfect copies of ideal forms that exist in the realm of pure spirit. With his *David,* he was concerned to represent both an archetypal beautiful body and a heroic character. In our own day we have seen that the ideals of human strength or beauty, rather than character, are presented in popular media. Some men and women become obsessed with appearance, believing that they will not be acceptable without perfectly formed and cultivated bodies. From a Christian perspective, this is a form of idolatry—worship of part of the creation rather than the Creator.

It is certainly good to care for our bodies, to exercise regularly and to eat healthy food, but our bodies do not last forever. Reluctant as we may be to admit it in this youth-oriented culture, between the ages of thirty and forty early signs of decay gradually begin to appear in the form of facial wrinkles, stiff joints, weak knees, aching backs and failing memories. The cosmetic and pharmaceutical industries know that there are many desperate men and women anxious to postpone the ravages of age with face lifts, Botox injections and pills for painful joints and declining brain power. Sooner or later we have to admit that except for a few ups now and then, it is basically down-hill all the way! (I speak from personal experience, as at my age there always seems to be some new ache with which to contend, and I have to work harder to keep fit.) Some people manage to remain healthy and strong to a ripe old age, but many others suffer all sorts of physical complaints and serious illnesses.

The Bible helps us keep things in perspective. Isaiah wrote rather bluntly, "All men are like grass, / and all their glory is like the flowers of the field. / The grass withers and the flowers fall" (Is 40:6-7). I often think of this verse when I see the beauty of the flowers in the arrangements my wife produces for weddings. Yet a few days later the color fades, and when the flowers begin to droop it is hard to remember how glorious they once were.

Looking to the future, Paul writes of a difference in the "splendor" or glory of our earthly bodies when compared to the glory of our resurrection bodies. Our current bodies, affected by sin, are subject to disease, decay and death. The resurrected body is "imperishable," glorious and powerful (1 Cor 15:40-50). Our present bodies are to be neither obsessed over nor ignored, neither loved too much nor hated, because they are temporary and one day will be more wonderful than they are now.[*]

So while we should not idolize human beauty, we also should not treat it as insignificant. The apostle Peter helps us keep a right perspective on the ultimate value of physical beauty: "Your beauty should not come [primarily] from outward adornment, such as . . . hair . . . jewelry and fine clothes. Instead, it should be that of your inner self, the unfading beauty of a gentle and quiet spirit, which is of great worth in God's sight" (1 Pet 3:3-4). Although physical beauty is a gift from God to be appreciated and enjoyed—as shown in the passionate and sensual poem of Song of Solomon, where the lover praises his beloved's beauty (Song 6:9)—it should not become the defining characteristic of a person's identity in the way it does in American culture today.

Physical strength is also a good thing, but strength and rippling muscles should not become too important. The psalmist says that God takes no "delight in the legs of a man" (Ps 147:10). "Physical training," says Paul, does have "some value" (1 Tim 4:8), but it is one among many priorities in life and should not become the main source of value or identity. Training the body is good, but "habits of the heart" are even more important.

---

[*]Concern with physical appearance and fitness is good, but we easily swing to all-or-nothing, perfectionist extremes of caring too much or not caring at all if we cannot be perfect.

It is interesting that God chose not to emphasize physical beauty in Jesus' appearance. He was not described as David was in the Old Testament as having a "fine appearance and handsome features" (1 Sam 16:12). Instead we read of the coming Messiah, "He had no beauty or majesty to attract us to him, / nothing in his appearance that we should desire him" (Is 53:2).

PERFORMANCE

If physical appearance is too highly valued in this culture, so is performance. We have to admit that we all want to impress others by getting straight A's, being honored as a prize-winning musician or outstanding athlete, or becoming the top artist, doctor or lawyer in town. As I mentioned in an earlier chapter, the Olympics give us a glimpse of the passionate pursuit of perfect performances. It is a wonderful thing to see the amazing God-given potential of the human body and mind. We are called to develop our abilities and talents, however small, as much as we can—to use our minds and creativity to reflect God's image in us, to develop and explore creation, and to pursue excellence in all areas of life. It is when our whole identity and value rests in the achievement of a perfect score that things begin to go wrong. The pursuit of excellence in performance is a wonderful thing, but only if it is kept in its place alongside other important character values. Aristotle said, "We are what we repeatedly do. Excellence then is not an act but a habit."

Brightest and best. In an article in *The Atlantic Monthly* titled "The Organization Kid," David Brooks described a visit to observe some of the brightest and best students at Princeton University. He interviewed a few dozen students and found that "at the top of the meritocratic ladder we have in America a generation of students who are extraordinarily bright, morally earnest, and incredibly industrious."[2†] As he talked to them, he realized that there was a huge difference between this and preceding generations in that "these students work harder, are more neatly groomed, and defer to their teachers more readily." They also seem to know how to achieve and how to succeed in order to live a particular lifestyle. He continues:

> The most striking contrast between that elite [previous generation] and this one is that its members were relatively unconcerned with academic achievement but went to enormous lengths to instill character. We, on the other hand, place enormous emphasis on achievement but are tongue-tied and hesitant when it comes to what makes for a virtuous life. . . . Today's students do not inherit a concrete and articulated moral system—a set of ideals to instruct privileged men and women on how to live, how to see their duties, and how to call upon their highest efforts. Although today's Princeton and today's parents impose all sorts of rules to reduce safety risks and encourage achievement, they do not go to great lengths to build character, the way adults and adult institutions did a century ago.

One result of this overemphasis on material success can be seen in the rash of wealthy business executives being charged with fraud and dishonesty. Since we are losing some of the old categories and concepts of character, moral integrity and long-term faithfulness in relationships, Brooks continues,

> it's hard to imagine what it would be like to be a saint, but it's

---

†There are many people, especially those not blessed with natural beauty, inherited wealth or great intelligence, who react with cynicism and apathy to the realization that it is hopeless to do more than dream of wealth and success. This is a different form of conformity—to the culture of the casual, cool and careless; it is a culture that embraces mediocrity, caring about little except immediate pleasure. Of course, there are many in between these extremes.

easy to see what it is to be a success. . . . They (the students) live in a country that has lost, in its frenetic seeking after happiness and success, the language of sin and character building through combat with sin. Evil is seen as something that can be cured with better education, or therapy, or Prozac. Instead of virtue we talk about accomplishment.[3]

THE IMPORTANCE OF CHARACTER

The perfection we should strive for is not found in appearance or performance. We should resist allowing ourselves to be squeezed into the mindset of the world around us. True perfection is found in developing a Christlike character. If we are pursuing excellence out of fear of rejection, self-centeredness or pride, then we are not moving toward maturity and perfection. We can seek to be the best that we can be, with all our intellectual and artistic abilities, but the motive is all-important. In the film *Chariots of Fire,* Eric Liddell runs in order to use his gift well, for the sheer joy of it, and out of love for his Creator. His chief rival, Abrahams, runs to prove that he is better than everyone else. He is motivated by insecurity, fear of failure and the desire to prove himself. His sense of value and identity depend on winning. "If I can't win," he says, "I won't run."

To be like Christ is to be truly human. This does not mean that we are to mirror Christ physically or match his intellectual abilities or lifestyle. Instead we are to reflect Christ's character in our attitudes and relationships. When Christ says, "Be perfect," he is encouraging us to make this our goal until we are finally made perfect in heaven. Jesus uses the word *perfect* not in relation to performance or appearance but in relation to *maturity* in personal development. For now, we must increasingly allow the fruits of the Spirit—love, joy, peace, patience, kindness, goodness, faithfulness, gentleness and self-control (Gal 5:22-23)—to grow in us. At the same time we must resist the fruits of our "sinful nature." All of us, but particularly perfectionists, have a tendency to be self-centered, proud, mistrustful, afraid, covetous and critical.

On toward maturity. We are called to a transformation of values and character. There are many lists of character virtues in Scripture. One such list is found in Jesus' teaching in the Sermon on the Mount. His list of virtues turns the values of the world upside down. Blessed, he said, are those who are poor in spirit, mournful (over their sin and the sin of the world), meek and gentle, hungry and thirsty for righteousness (not for a perfect body or house), merciful, pure in heart, peacemakers, and those persecuted because of their goodness (Mt 5:3-10). Paul exhorts the Colossian believers to a life of union with Christ that is expressed in being compassionate, kind, humble, gentle, patient, forgiving and thankful (Col 3:12-15). These are difficult virtues for the perfectionist. For example, there seems to be little to be thankful for when things could always be better, and when people do not live up to their own standards, impatience is not far beneath the surface.

In the biblical stories, we also see some virtues that are not listed above. Jesus, for example, was sometimes surprisingly tough and assertive in the face of evil. Paul stood up for his rights as a Roman citizen when he was about to be beaten (Acts 22:22-29). It would be wrong to think of Christians as spineless and weak people who allow themselves to be walked over or used. Some perfectionists have a strong desire to please others and may have a hard time asserting themselves in a healthy way. Yet the virtues that Jesus and Paul talk about are not just external actions but deep habits of the heart.

A DOUBLE BIND?

You may be feeling the tension of an apparent contradiction. I am telling you to try harder to be a better person, yet earlier I was saying that you can't do it yourself, you have to rely on God. The Bible says that we are to "be perfect," but it also says we cannot be good enough for God. However "perfectly" we try to be perfect, failing again and again to live up to our own standards, let alone God's, is certainly our experience. Does this feel like a double bind in which whatever we do is wrong?

When you become a Christian you are given the moral perfection of Christ. God will no longer reject or punish you for your imperfections. The righteousness and perfection of Christ covers those imperfections, and you are now part of God's family forever (2 Cor 5:21). This is God's grace (Eph 2:1-10). It is as if the judge ruled that you are guilty of murder. You were sentenced to die, but someone else, Christ, stepped in and took your place and has been punished instead of you. So now you are free from condemnation. Isaiah's prophecy of Christ's death puts it clearly: "He was pierced for our transgressions, he was crushed for our iniquities; the punishment that brought us peace was upon him, and by his wounds we are healed" (Is 53:5). The consequence of this amazing gift is that now we should desire to change not out of fear but out of gratitude and love, as God works with us to be more like him—not in physical appearance or intellectual ability, but in character.[†]

So at one level you are seen by God as perfect already (justified), but at another level he knows that you are still imperfect and need to be perfected (sanctified). Martin Luther wrote:

This life, therefore, is not righteousness but growth in right-

---

[†]For a deeper understanding of this key theme of grace, I recommend Philip Yancey, *What's So Amazing About Grace?* (Grand Rapids: Zondervan, 1997); Bryan Chapell, *Holiness by Grace* (Wheaton, Ill.: Crossway, 2001); and for both children and adults, Max Lucado's *You Are Special* (Wheaton, Ill.: Crossway, 2000).

eousness, not health but healing, not being but becoming, not
rest but exercise; we are not yet what we shall be, but we are
growing toward it; the process is not yet finished, but it is going
on; this is not the end, but it is the road.[4]

You are being changed, but there are many things that will not be
changed this side of heaven, and there are many things that we do not
like about our finiteness and fragility in this world that we have to learn
to accept. Another virtue, contentment, becomes very important when
living with incompleteness and imperfection. "Godliness with contentment is great gain," writes Paul (1 Tim 6:6). Contentment is not the
same as laziness or sloth, but it is something that perfectionists find
very hard to experience because they are always dissatisfied and pursuing more. Trusting that God is good and in control frees us from the
pressure to right every wrong, heal every hurt and reach every goal.

This transformation of character is a slow and sometimes painful
process. We are obstinate creatures, and perfectionists are especially
fearful of and resistant to change. They want to remain in control of
their own lives. Giving up control and learning to trust that God is in
ultimate control is scary. But in the context of relationships God
works to rub off the sharp corners and to make us more like himself,
more perfectly human, more trusting.

In the story of *The Velveteen Rabbit* we meet the toys in a children's
nursery. The old Skin Horse, we are told, was balding and showing
some of his seams. His tail was thin where children had pulled the
hairs to string bead necklaces. He had seen many other toys come
and eventually break their mainsprings and pass on, but being old
and wise he knew about the "strange and wonderful" nursery magic.

"What is REAL?" asked the Rabbit one day, when they were lying side by side near the nursery fender. . . . "Does it mean hav-

ing things that buzz inside you and a stick-out-handle [appearance and performance]?"

"Real isn't how you are made," said the Skin Horse. "It's a thing that happens to you. When a child loves you for a long, long time, not just to play with, but REALLY loves you, then you become Real."

"Does it hurt?" asked the Rabbit.

"Sometimes," said the Skin Horse, for he was always truthful. "When you are Real you don't mind being hurt."

"Does it happen all at once, like being wound up," he asked, "or bit by bit?"

"It doesn't happen all at once," said the Skin Horse. "You become. It takes a long time. That's why it doesn't often happen to people who break easily, or have sharp edges, or who have to be carefully kept. Generally, by the time you are Real, most of your hair has been loved off, and your eyes drop out and you get loose in the joints and very shabby. But these things don't matter at all, because once you are Real you can't be ugly, except to people who don't understand."[5]

Mature human beings are more like soft, worn-out, stuffed animals than like hard, brittle, mechanical toys that can be made to look shiny and bright and perform well but easily break. Perfectionists often seem more like those good-looking, mechanical toys. Over time, however, a slow but sure mellowing and humanizing can take place, if they are willing to take the risk of being involved in relationships, letting go of control and allowing God to work to change them. They become more like God wants them to be: more human, more real, more like the only perfect human—Christ!

In the movie *Mostly Martha,* Martha is a chef at a high-end German restaurant. She lives a lonely but ordered existence in her immaculate apartment. She is regarded as one of the best chefs in town. She has a very hard time sharing her inner world with people (even her psycho-therapist) and takes refuge in the more familiar and secure arena of rec-ipes and food. Her perfectionism serves her well in her job most of the time ("I'm not obsessive," she says, "I'm just precise"), but she tends to fly off the handle at the slightest criticism of the food she has so care-fully prepared. Then her world is turned upside down by her sister's death, and Martha finds herself caring for her grieving, unhappy, eight-year-old niece. This relationship is tense, and after one particularly dif-ficult moment, Martha's life script is poignantly revealed as she says to little Lena: "I wish I had a recipe for you that I could follow." Her per-fectionism is then further disrupted by a delightful, relaxed Italian chef with whom she now has to share her kitchen at the restaurant. In the context of these two challenging relationships, we see the beginning of a transformation as Martha's warmth, fun and humanness are drawn out. A new reality tests the priority of her rigid routines.[6]

In the Grip of Grace

There is a final biblical example of a perfectionist who had his values turned upside down. In Philippians 3 the apostle Paul wrote that if anyone had anything, in terms of racial and religious background, to impress people in the culture in which he lived, he had it all. In terms of his record of keeping the law and being a righteous person, he was "faultless." His performance was impeccable. He was the "perfect" Jew—or so he thought. All this, he came to realize, was "rubbish" compared to knowing Christ and relying totally on his righteousness for acceptance and identity. Nothing that Paul could do would earn his own acceptance by God. He wrote: "Not having a righteousness of my own . . . but . . . the righteousness that comes from God and is by faith" (Phil 3:9). Paul knew that he was not perfected in this life because he followed with: "Not that I have already obtained all this, or have already been made perfect, but I press on to take hold of that for which Christ Jesus took hold of me" (Phil 3:12).

That is finally *our* greatest comfort; Christ has us in his grip, and somehow he will complete the task of making us perfect and bringing us to glory. When we fail we can let ourselves off the hook of continual self-recrimination because Christ accepts us as we are. We can serve him, love him and obey him, not out of terror that one day we might not be good enough but because we know he loves us so profoundly and is working in us to transform us day by day. Paul prayed that God would "sanctify [us] through and through," knowing that, when Christ returns, our whole being, "spirit, soul and body," will be renewed completely (1 Thess 5:23).

Paul's priorities were changed from his earlier years when he passionately, and obsessively, wanted to perform and impress. After he saw the light (literally on the road to Damascus!) he wanted, above all things, to "know Christ" and to become like him. He moved from preoccupation with performance to deep concern about his relationship with God and with the people around him. Knowing God's love and purpose for him, he was able to learn "the secret of being content in any and every situation" (Phil 4:12). But he was deeply aware of his imperfection and his need of transformation, for he said, "We eagerly await a Savior . . . , the Lord Jesus Christ, who, by the power that enables him to bring everything under his control, will transform our lowly bodies so that they will be like his glorious body" (Phil 3:20-21). Christ is in control, and we—our bodies, minds and emotions—will be mysteriously and wonderfully changed. Then, and only then, will we have finally reached our goal: maturity, perfection and glory. C. S. Lewis, again, puts it so well:

He meant what he said. Those who put themselves in His hands will become perfect, as He is perfect—perfect in love, wisdom, joy, beauty, and immortality. The change will not be completed in this life, for death is an important part of the treatment. How far the change will have gone before death in any particular Christian is uncertain.[7]

God has promised that our dreams of glory and hopes of perfection will one day be fulfilled when Christ returns. But the renewal of creation will probably not conform to our stereotypical images of perfection. It will be far richer, more diverse and more wonderful than we can imagine. Then we will be free at last to be who we truly are without the tension and striving of our present existence. It is hard to wait for that day, but we are being changed and we must live step by step, a day at a time until the day when we are completely set free from the chains of imperfection. With Paul we groan, waiting eagerly and patiently, like a woman in labor, for the pain to be past and the joy of a new life to begin (Rom 8:18-24). In the meantime we resist the tyranny of unhealthy perfectionism by living in the understanding of God's total acceptance of us, imperfect as we are, daily strengthened by the Spirit of God working in us and with the anticipation that in the world to come there will be no failures, no shame, no guilt and no fear of disapproval or rejection. Then we will stand amazed as we delight in the wonder of that perfection—a mystery at last revealed in all its glory!

QUESTIONS FOR DISCUSSION

1. How concerned should we be about how we look?
2. How concerned should we be about success and achievement, and about ambition to do or be the best?

3. What is the perfection that we should strive for?

4. How is it that God demands that we be perfect and yet accepts us as very imperfect people?

5. Is it possible to pursue excellence and avoid the perils of perfectionism?

6. Why is grace the key that unlocks the prison of unhealthy perfectionism?

APPENDIX

Perfectionism in History and Religion

Throughout history we have dreamed of improving and perfecting ourselves. Plato, Karl Marx, B. F. Skinner and others have written of utopian societies. In this appendix I summarize the history of the pursuit of individual perfection in ancient Greece, Christianity, Hinduism and Buddhism, with the hope that this will help to put our discussion of perfectionism in contemporary culture in a larger context.

IDEAS OF PERFECTION IN ANCIENT GREECE

Plato believed that for every thing in our world there was a perfect, or ideal, form or template. This concept is called metaphysical perfection. For a physical object, like a chair or table, there exists an ideal form of that object somewhere in the universe. For a personal being, there is an ideal, perfect, Supreme Being—and some human beings can share the metaphysical perfection of the Supreme Being. Aristotle believed that ultimate peace of mind and perfection were acquired through the development of the highest part of his being, his reason, and by acquiring intellectual knowledge.[1] This was later taken up and elaborated by Thomas Aquinas within a Christian worldview. Plato believed that only an elite few could achieve such refined perfection through education, by withdrawing from the world or by living in a perfect society. He also held that most people cannot attain such levels of knowledge and, therefore, remain imperfect and have a lower level of morality.[2]

This ideal that Plato and, centuries later, the philosopher Immanuel Kant believed in was not arbitrary or relative. It was somehow a given in the order of things and had to be discovered by humans. Jews and Muslims believe that God has given us the ideal in written form in the sacred scriptures of the Torah and the Qur'an. The Christian believes that God has given it in written form in the Bible and in personal form by coming to this earth as a perfect human being. So the most fundamental disagreement between the Greek and the Jewish, Christian and Muslim views is whether we are left on our own to discover or create the ideal, the standard of perfection, or whether it has already been given to us. John Passmore, philosopher and author, points out that

> in some ways, the most influential Jewish idea of all, and the least Greek, was the idea of a sacred book, holy scriptures, a solitary and complete source of revelation, given by God to Moses. . . . This was to act as a permanent restraint on Christian, as on Muslim, theological speculation. . . . Christian disputes about perfectibility, therefore, are in part—in a manner very disconcerting to a philosopher—a battle of texts. The true view, it is presumed, must at least be consistent with what has been revealed in Scripture, and ought, in so fundamental a matter, to be deducible from it.[3]

CHRISTIANITY AND PERFECTIONISM

Christianity grew from its original Jewish roots into a cultural environment heavily influenced by Greek ideas. Most Christians equate perfection with sinlessness, and there have been many debates through the centuries about whether or not it is possible to achieve such perfection in this life. Jesus taught his disciples that they should be as perfect as his Father in heaven. A few interpreted this to mean that perfection was possible in this life, and they worked very hard to achieve it. The majority interpreted this command, in the context of the rest of Scripture, to be something to aim for rather than a goal that could be achieved in this life.

However, the core of Christian teaching is that human beings, although created in the image of God and retaining some remnants of that glory and dignity, are thoroughly corrupt, sinful and unlike God, and so cannot hope to achieve perfection by their own efforts. Both the Hebrew Scripture and the New Testament stress the greatness and holiness of God in contrast to the smallness and sinfulness of human beings.

Yet the early Christians couldn't escape the influence of Greek thought. Passmore writes:

> Gnosticism has been a constant temptation to Christianity: the view, at least, that Christians could perfect themselves, if once they were prepared to withdraw from the world, to mortify the body, and thus to soar above the flesh is one which constantly recurs in Christian thinking.[4]

Early church fathers. Passmore quotes Clement of Alexandria who taught that "the 'perfected Gnostic', the man who has reached the heights of Christian knowledge, is 'assimilated to God', he has 'undisturbed intercourse and communion with the Lord', he is 'translated absolutely and entirely to another sphere.'" [5] This could be achieved by perfect obedience to the commandments. Clement said, "He who holds conversation with God must have his soul immaculate and pure, without stain. It is essential to have made himself perfectly good."[6] Clement's pupil, Origen, again with strong Platonic influence, taught that perfection could be achieved by a rejection of the external world, the emotions, the body and the sex drive. Only a few enlightened people achieve such a level of existence. Dionysius, in the fifth century, asserted that men can be perfected and even deified. He had an enormous influence on medieval theology, and his writings have been called "a charter of Christian mysticism."[7] (Martin Luther later condemned the teachings of Dionysius as " 'pure fables and lies' and 'sheer nonsense,' the work of a man who is quite obviously a disciple of Plato, not of Christ."[8])

In the fifth century a British monk, Pelagius, attacked Augustine's view that man cannot reach perfection in this life. Pelagius believed that God would not tell us to do something that's beyond our reach. He denied the doctrine of original sin and taught that people are born with "a capacity for perfecting themselves or corrupting themselves, by the exercise of their free-will."[9] Augustine responded with a series of tracts emphasizing human corruption and the necessity of divine grace to enable us to have a relationship with God and begin to be changed in the direction of perfection. Augustine affirmed the ideal of perfection as the greatest good but taught that it was only reached in eternity.

Throughout the centuries, theologians, in the Augustinian tradition, have emphasized the foundational sin of pride, the belief that we do not need God's help and grace to become who we are supposed to be.

Monasticism. Some monks followed the path of good works, poverty and chastity in order to achieve perfection. Others followed the path of a more complete renunciation of the world and retreated into deserts or monasteries to pray and contemplate God. Passmore writes that some took this to the extreme: "renunciation of every form of human love in the quest for the vision of God."[10] "That is why Teresa of Avila was so alarmed to discover that she loved her sister above other women and was deeply concerned about her unhappiness. In Teresa's eyes, this was a sure proof that she was still not perfect, still not 'entirely detached,' still not wholly given to God."[11] In the Catholic Church, this inevitably gave rise to an elite group of mystics and ascetics who attempted to reach a pure state of freedom from sin and union with God by a life of contemplation, chastity and absolute simplicity (ordinary people lived at the level of obedience to the Church and the commandments but did not achieve such exalted states).

Reformers. Luther and Calvin were each critical of such monasticism and ascetic ideals, believing that perfection was impossible. "Christians who try to bring themselves to such a state of perfection as to be 'without all feelings of temptations and sins' are trying to reduce themselves, Luther argues, to the state of 'sticks and stones.'"[12] What characterized the monks and mystics was the belief that they could, by their own efforts, suppress the carnal passions of the body, detach themselves from the world and thus achieve a state of purity of being. The reformers followed the Augustinian view that sin remains in the believer until he is made perfect by God beyond death. Calvin writes:

> Only let us look toward our mark with sincere simplicity and aspire to our goal; not fondly flattering ourselves, nor excusing our own evil deeds, but with continuous effort striving toward this end: that we may surpass ourselves in goodness until we obtain goodness itself. . . . But we shall attain it only when we

have cut off the weakness of the body, and are received into full fellowship with him.[13]

Christian mysticism. With the Quakers and Methodists, a different sort of mysticism and perfectionism arose in the Protestant church of later centuries. George Fox, in 1659, claimed that God had taken away all his sin, and therefore, he was perfect. He explained in a letter to Oliver Cromwell, written in 1654, that because he had experienced a rebirth, he was no longer that sinful man born George Fox; now that he had Christ dwelling in him, he was a new and sinless man.[14] James Nayler, a disciple of George Fox, was imprisoned for his heretical views, and after his release he rode into Bristol in a manner reminiscent of Christ entering Jerusalem, surrounded by the hosannas of a small band of disciples. Passmore writes: "Charged with blasphemy, he said of his worshippers that they were to blame if they were worshipping the visible James Nayler, but not if they were worshipping the invisible Christ within. The court was unimpressed, and Nayler was severely punished."[15]

John Wesley and Methodism. John Wesley, the founder of Methodism, believed that Christians could achieve sinless perfection. In his *Plain Account of Christian Perfection,* we see the development of his teaching from 1725 to 1777. He believed that we should seek a "holiness which frees the soul from all sin and endows it with Christ's virtues, so that it can truly be said to be 'perfect as our Father in heaven is perfect.'"[16] He later claimed that the perfected Christian will "want for nothing; he will not even ask for ease from pain; he will never doubt what to do; he will never be troubled by temptation . . . 'one in whom is no occasion of stumbling, and who accordingly does not commit sin.' "[17] One of his hymns sums up the theme: "He walks in glorious liberty, to sin entirely dead." He believed that God changes our sinful nature so that we can live a life of perfect love. It is an affirmation of God's grace and power to transform us into his image. Wesley himself never claimed to have achieved this state of "perfect love" and, at times, wondered along with his brother, Charles, whether it would be wise to omit this teaching from Methodism. Later, John Wesley wrote of the possibility of committing involuntary transgressions, arising out of ignorance, and of the need, therefore, for Christians to still pray for forgiveness. Reality eventually impinged on his world, and when surrounded by instances of Christian sinfulness, he reluctantly admitted that it was possible to fall away from perfection.[18] He was very aware of the great dangers of his teaching: pride on the one hand, antinomianism (the belief that, with faith, one is no longer bound to keep the commandments) on the other hand. The latter led to the belief that whatever one did, even if obviously sinful, was perfect.

A similar tradition of perfectionism was a strong influence in the evangelical church in the nineteenth and early twentieth centuries through such preachers as Charles Finney and Robert Pearsall Smith.[19] The influence continues today in some Free Methodist, Nazarene and Pentecostal churches, as well as in revivalism and the holiness movement. It was also an influence on William Booth's teaching in the Salvation Army. The term *perfection* is often avoided by these groups, being replaced by "entire sanctification."

Ranters, Shakers and other groups. Other groups through the ages have claimed perfection. The leader of the Montanists in the second century claimed to be God in human form. Some of the Brethren of the Free Spirit, who flourished in Europe between the twelfth and sixteenth centuries, believed that they had "advanced in perfection beyond God, of whom they no longer had any need."[20] The English branch, called the Ranters, gave themselves permission for all sorts of immorality, because they held that "there is no act whatsoever, that is impure in God, or sinful with or before God."[21] To counter this extraordinary view, in 1650 the House of Commons passed a law "for 'the Punishment of Atheistical, Blasphemous and Execrable Opinions' which laid down penalties for those who professed that 'acts of adultery, drunkenness, swearing . . . are in their own nature as holy and righteous as the duties of prayer, preaching, or giving thanks to God.'"[22]

Christian Scientists, the Shakers, the Universalists and the Mormons, all, at one time or another, had perfectionist tendencies. Joseph Smith, the American Mormon prophet, said in a funeral oration: "You have got to learn how to be Gods yourselves."[23] Many Eastern cults, the Church of Scientology, the Unification Church of Sun Myung Moon and various types of Transpersonal psychology teach that we can perfect ourselves through our own efforts, by spiritual disciplines or by mystical techniques that enable adherents to realize their inherent godlikeness and perfection here and now.

We have seen, therefore, that for many centuries a belief in the possibility of achieving perfection in this life and by one's own efforts has been a seductive temptation for branches of the Christian church.

HINDUISM AND BUDDHISM

One of the key differences between Hinduism, Buddhism and Christianity is that Hinduism and Buddhism focus on getting rid of personality and individuality in order to become perfect. The goal is becoming one with the divine or the cosmos—"returning to the One from which they had emanated."[24] Christianity, by contrast, emphasizes more truly becoming the human being that you were made to be—in the image of God, with a separate personal individuality and identity, able to enter into relationship with a personal, infinite God.

Christians do not become *God in essence,* they become what God made them to be, *like God in character.*

Hinduism teaches that ultimate reality is absolute perfection. *Brahman,* the absolute, cannot be described in human categories. Buddhism discards all notions of deity but teaches that ultimate reality is *nirvana,* the state of blissful purity and enlightenment, or *dharma,* the eternal truth beneath everything.

Hinduism and Buddhism teach that human beings fall short of this perfection in three ways. First, we are ignorant of the fact that we are, in reality, one with Brahman already and therefore perfect. Second, because we are ignorant of our true state, we act in foolish ways by becoming too attached to appearances of things, thus generating wrong desires. Third, we may only be liberated from our false view of reality, to experience nirvana or oneness with Brahman, through many reincarnations or through experiences of instantaneous or gradual enlightenment.

To achieve perfection, the Hindu and Buddhist traditions set out several paths. Both teach an ethical path of right actions and a mystical path of concentration and meditation. Enlightened beings achieve a state of perfection in which they overcome ignorance, sensuality, desire, pride and egocentricity. Some sects put more emphasis on the achievement of mystical enlightenment and realization of one's essential divinity and perfection; others recognize the need for discipline and acts of kindness and love to achieve perfection. Certain individuals, gurus, Buddhist *siddhas, arhats* and others are held up as examples of ordinary individuals whose lives are "charged with the transcendent and supernatural."[25] These "siddhas are depicted as having attained full awakening . . . 'enlightenment in this very lifetime.' "[26] It is said that these early siddhas carried the teaching of Buddhism to Tibet, China, Japan and Southeast Asia. In Buddhist writings "the arhat is described as one who is free from desire, hatred, and delusion, who knows everything, and who is endowed with miraculous powers."[27] The influence of this form of Buddhism has spread to Sri Lanka, Burma and Thailand.

In the tradition of Confucianism, there is the concept of *chen-jen,* a "real" or "perfect person." This person, by various disciplines, has "preserved original purity and integrity," gotten rid of "perverse energies" and achieved a state of immortality and supernatural powers. This Taoist master or mistress becomes the one who "transmits the sacred secrets."[28]

Individual initiative in achieving perfection is the main emphasis in Buddhist and Hindu teaching, but there are also some hints of the possibility of divine initiative, which is somewhat comparable to the Christian idea of grace. For Hindus there is the way of *bhakti,* devotion to a god who will help the worshiper achieve perfection. The Pure Land sect of Mahayana Buddhism teaches that, since the path of meditative purification is too difficult for most people, it is only necessary to invoke the mercy and grace of Amida Buddha to be "saved" and given perfection.

CONCLUSION

Anders Nygren has summarized four aspects of religion in relation to perfection. First, religion reveals the perfection of ultimate reality, the eternal, in concepts of wholeness, completeness and integrity. Second, in contrast to this perfect, ultimate reality stands the imperfect nature of human beings. Third, religion provides a way to bridge the gap and achieve reconciliation between the divine and the human by initiative from either side. The final result is the possibility of the union of the soul with the eternal. In Hinduism the end goal is realization of one's essential divinity.[29] In Buddhism it is realization of one's oneness with all that is. In Christianity it is realization of one's imperfection and separation from God and the need for a means of restoration of relationship with God. Robert Cohn, writing on the concept of sainthood in world religions, states: "The boundary between humanity and divinity is far more fluid in Hinduism and Eastern religions generally than it is in the monotheistic faiths."[30]

In Christianity the gap between divinity and humanity is caused initially by our finiteness (we are not God) and, after the Fall, by sin. There is also a metaphysical and moral distance. We will never be like God or be one with him in our finiteness, but the broken relationship because of sin and moral imperfection can be healed. Eastern mysticism speaks of "at-one-ment" to describe our relationship with God. We can be one with him in essence and character. The Christian knows that we need a different sort of atonement (a sacrifice for sin), and that is why a cross is the main symbol of Christianity. Christianity looks back to the real, historical event of Christ's death and resurrection because it restored the possibility of relationship with the infinite, personal and loving God. It gave the promise of a future perfection where all the disorder, disease and destruction that came into the world because of sin will be removed or healed. Something happened two thousand years ago that changed the world forever, bringing healing and hope instead of sickness and cynicism.

NOTES

Chapter 1: The Seductive Sirens of Perfectionism

[1] Lexus LS430 advertisement, *New York Times*, 25 June 2002, p. 12.

[2] Michael Sandel, "The Case Against Perfection," *Atlantic Monthly*, April 2004, pp. 51-62.

[3] Gregory Stock, *Redesigning Humans: Our Inevitable Genetic Future* (Boston: Houghton Mifflin, 2002).

[4] Gina Maranto, *Quest for Perfection: The Drive to Breed Better Human Beings* (New York: Scribner, 1996).

[5] Gina Maranto, "Deoxyribonucleic Acid Trip," review of *Our Inevitable Genetic Future,* by Gregory Stock, *New York Times Book Review,* 25 August 2002, p. 25.

[6] Quoted by Bill Keller in "Charlie's Ghost," *New York Times* op-ed, 29 June 2002, A27.

[7] Miriam Elliot and Susan Meltsner, *The Perfectionist Predicament: How to Stop Driving Yourself and Others Crazy* (New York: William Morrow, 1991), pp. 11-12.

[8] *The New Shorter Oxford English Dictionary,* 4th ed., s.v. "perfect"; *Webster's Third New International,* s.v. "perfect."

[9] *Random House Unabridged Dictionary,* 2nd ed., s.v. "perfection."

[10] Robert K. Barnhart, ed., *The Barnhart Dictionary of Etymology* (New York: H. W. Wilson Co., 1988), s.v. "perfectionist."

Chapter 2: The Pursuit of Excellence

[1] Gordon L. Flett and Paul L. Hewitt, "Perfectionism and Maladjustment: An Overview of Theoretical, Definitional, and Treatment Issues," in *Perfectionism: Theory, Research, and Treatment,* ed. Gordon Flett and Paul Hewitt (Washington, D.C.: American Psychological Association, 2002), p. 5.

[2] Miriam Adderholdt, *Perfectionism: What's so Bad About Being Too Good?* (Minneapolis: Free Spirit Publishing Company, 1987).

[3] Don Hamachek, "Psychodynamics of Normal and Neurotic Perfectionism," *Psychology* 15 (1978): 27.

[4] L. K. Silverman, "Perfectionism" (paper presented at the 11th Conference on Gifted and Talented Children, Hong Kong, 1995), 1.

[5] Peter Bieling, Anne Israeli and Martin Antony, "Is Perfectionism Good, Bad or Both? Examin-

ing Models of the Perfectionism Construct," *Personality and Individual Differences* 36 (2004): 1373-85

[6]Hamachek, "Psychodynamics," p. 27.

[7]Marc Hollender, "Perfectionism," *Comprehensive Psychiatry* 6, no. 2 (1965): 96.

[8]Flett and Hewitt, "Perfectionism and Maladjustment," p.18.

[9]Thomas S. Greenspon, *Freeing Our Families from Perfectionism* (Minneapolis: Free Spirit Publishing, 2001).

[10]Robert Hill, Karen McIntire and Verne Bacharach, "Perfectionism and the Big Five Factors," *Journal of Social Behavior and Personality* 12, no. 1 (1997): 257-70.

[11]See Paul T. Costa Jr. and Robert R. McCrae, *NEO Personality Inventory—Revised* (Lutz, Fla.: Psychological Assessment Resources, 1992); or see <www.mrs.umn.edu/~ratliffj/big_five.htm>.

[12]"Can our Personality Change Over Time?" *The Meninger Letter* 3, no. 3 (1995): 7. See also Paul T. Costa Jr. and Thomas A. Widiger, eds., *Personality Disorders and the Five-Factor Model of Personality* (Washington, D.C.: American Psychological Association, 1994).

[13]Flett and Hewitt, "Perfectionism and Maladjustment," p. 18.

[14]David Stoop, *Hope for the Perfectionist* (Nashville: Thomas Nelson, 1991). Used with permission.

[15]Wayne Parker and Carol Mills, "The Incidence of Perfectionism in Gifted Students," *The Gifted Child Quarterly* 40, no. 4 (1996): 194.

[16]Jonathan Gaston, Danielle Einstein and Peter Lovibond, "Relationship Between Perfectionism and Emotional Symptoms in an Adolescent Sample," *Australian Journal of Psychology* 52, no. 2 (2000): 89-93. Perfectionist adolescents who perceived "strong external pressure to excel academically" were "at risk of severe emotional symptoms under examination stress."

[17]Parker and Mills, "Incidence of Perfectionism," p. 199.

[18]Sidney J. Blatt, "The Destructiveness of Perfectionism: Implications for the Treatment of Depression," *American Psychologist* 50, no. 12 (1995): 1003.

[19]Ibid., p. 1004

[20]Ibid.

[21]Michael Isikoff, "Foster was Shopping for a Private Lawyer, Probers Find," *Washington Post*, August 15, 1993, sec. A.

[22]Blatt, "The Destructiveness of Perfectionism," p. 1004

[23]E. Troy Higgins, "Self-Discrepancy: A Theory Relating Self and Affect," *Psychological Review* 94 (1987): 319-40.

[24]Robert B. Slaney and Jeffrey S. Ashby, "Perfectionism: Study of a Criterion Group," *Journal of Counseling and Development* 74 (1996): 393-98.

Chapter 3: Types of Perfectionism

[1]Miriam Elliott and Susan Meltsner, *The Perfectionist Predicament: How to Stop Driving Yourself and Others Crazy* (New York: William Morrow, 1991), pp. 5-6.

[2]David Burns, "The Perfectionist's Script for Self-Defeat," *Psychology Today*, November 1980, p. 37.

[3]Ibid.

[4]Randy O. Frost and Katherine J. Henderson, "Perfectionism and Reactions to Athletic Competition," *Journal of Sport and Exercise Psychology* 13 (1991): 323-35, quoted in Nathalie Koivula, Peter Hassman and Johan Fallby, "Self-Esteem and Perfectionism in Elite Athletes: Effects on Competitive Anxiety and Self-Confidence," *Personality and Individual Differences* 32, no. 5 (2002): 865-75.

[5]Paul L. Hewitt and Gordon L. Flett, "Perfectionism in the Self and Social Contexts: Conceptualization, Assessment, and Association with Psychopathology," *Journal of Personality and Social Psychology* 60, no. 3 (1991): 456-70.

[6]Gordon Flett et al., "Dimensions of Perfectionism and Type A Behavior," *Personality and Individual Differences* 16 (1994): 477-85.

[7]A. Marie Habke and Carol A. Flynn, "Interpersonal Aspects of Trait Perfectionism," in *Perfectionism: Theory, Research, and Treatment,* ed. Gordon L. Flett and Paul L. Hewitt (Washington, D.C.: American Psychological Association, 2002), p. 159.

[8]Kris Henning, Sydney Ey and Darlene Shaw, "Perfectionism, the Impostor Phenomenon and Psychological Adjustment in Medical, Dental, Nursing and Pharmacy Students," *Medical Education* 32, no. 5 (1998): 456. Interestingly, the health profession students, contrary to expectation, did not report more perfectionism than students in other fields.

[9]Prem S. Fry, "Perfectionism, Humor, and Optimism as Moderators of Health Outcomes and Determinants of Coping Styles of Women Executives," *Genetic, Social and General Psychology Monographs* 121, no. 2 (1995): 211-45.

[10]Randy Frost et al., "The Dimensions of Perfectionism," *Cognitive Therapy and Research* 14, no. 5 (1990): 449-68. See also a new scale combining the main constructs of the two MPS scales in Robert Hill et al., "A New Measure of Perfectionism: A Perfectionism Inventory," *Journal of Personality Assessment* 82, no. 1 (2004): 80-91.

[11]Robert Slaney et al., "The Revised Almost Perfect Scale," *Measurement and Evaluation in Counseling and Development* 34, no. 3 (2001): 130-46.

Chapter 4: Depression, Anger and Eating Disorders

[1]Robert M. Lynd-Stevenson and Christie M. Hearne, "Perfectionism and Depressive Affect: The Pros and Cons of Being a Perfectionist," *Personality and Individual Differences* 26, no. 3 (1999): 549-62.

[2]Karen Kittler Adkins and Wayne Parker, "Perfectionism and Suicidal Preoccupation," *Journal of Personality* 64, no. 2 (1996): 539.

[3]Paul Hewitt, Gordon L. Flett and Evelyn Ediger, "Perfectionism and Depression: Longitudinal Assessment of a Specific Vulnerability Hypothesis," *Journal of Abnormal Psychology* 105, no. 2 (1996): 276-80.

[4]Gordon L. Flett et al., "Perfectionism, Life Events, and Depressive Symptoms: A Test of a Diathesis-Stress Model," *Current Psychology: Research and Reviews* 14, no. 2 (1995): 112-37.

[5]Paul Hewitt et al., "Perfectionism in Chronic and State Symptoms of Depression," *Canadian Journal of Behavioural Science* 30, no. 4 (1998): 235.

[6]Julian C. Hughes, "Wittgenstein's Dysphoria," *Integrative Psychiatry* 9 (1993): 88.

[7]E. Shulman, "Vulnerabilty Factors in Sylvia Plath's Suicide," *Death Studies* 22, no. 7 (1998): 597-613.

[8]Evan Thomas, John Barry and Gregory L. Vistica, "A Matter of Honor," *Newsweek*, May 27, 1996, pp. 24-29.

[9]Ann F. Garland and Edward Zigler, "Adolescent Suicide Prevention: Current Research and Social Policy Implications," *American Psychologist* 48, no. 2 (1993): 173.

[10]Sidney J. Blatt, "The Destructiveness of Perfectionism: Implications for the Treatment of Depression," *American Psychologist* 50, no. 12 (1995): 1005.

[11]Jeffrey Ashby, Terry Kottman and Eva Schoen, "Perfectionism and Eating Disorders Reconsidered," *Journal of Mental Health Counseling* 20, no. 3 (1998): 261-71; Katherine Halmi et al., "Perfectionism in Anorexia Nervosa: Variation by Clinical Subtype, Obsessionality, and

Pathological Eating Behavior," *American Journal of Psychiatry* 157, no. 11 (2000): 1799-805.

[12]Hilde Bruch, *The Golden Cage: The Enigma of Anorexia Nervosa* (Cambridge, Mass.: Harvard University Press, 1978), quoted in Elliot Goldner, Sarah Cockell and Suja Srikameswaran, "Perfectionism and Eating Disorders," in *Perfectionism: Theory, Research, and Treatment*, ed. Gordon Flett and Paul Hewitt (Washington, D.C.: American Psychological Association, 2002), pp. 320-21.

[13]Paul Hewitt, Gordon Flett and Evelyn Ediger, "Perfectionism Traits and Perfectionistic Self-Presentation in Eating Disorder Attitudes, Characteristics, and Symptoms," *International Journal of Eating Disorders* 18, no. 4 (1995): 317-26.

[14]Ibid., p. 322.

[15]Caroline Davis, "Normal and Neurotic Perfectionism in Eating Disorders: An Interactive Model," *The International Journal of Eating Disorders* 22, no. 4 (1997): 426. This study compared recovered anorexic women with healthy women and found that the women who had been anorectic had more obsessive-compulsive traits, along with more concerns about symmetry and the exact size of their bodies, than the "healthy" group, even after recovery.

[16]Goldner, Cockell and Srikameswaran, "Perfectionism and Eating Disorders," p. 320.

Chapter 5: Worry, Anxiety and Obsessions

[1]Martin Anthony et al., "Dimensions of Perfectionism across the Anxiety Disorders," *Behaviour Research and Therapy* 36, no. 12 (1998): 1143-54; Fredrik Saboonchi and Lars-Gunnar Lundh, "Perfectionism, Self-Consciousness and Anxiety," *Personality and Individual Differences* 22, no. 6 (1997): 921-28.

[2]Howard Hall, Alistair Kerr and Julie Matthews, "Precompetitive Anxiety in Sport: The Contribution of Achievement Goals and Perfectionism," *Journal of Sport & Exercise Psychology* 20, no. 2 (1998): 194-217; Randy Frost and Katherine Henderson, "Perfectionism and Reactions to Athletic Competition," *Journal of Sport & Exercise Psychology* 13 (1991): 323-35.

[3]Miriam Elliott and Susan Meltsner, *The Perfectionist Predicament: How to Stop Driving Yourself and Others Crazy* (New York: William Morrow, 1991), p. 108.

[4]Gordon Flett et al., "Perfectionism, Social Problem-Solving Ability, and Psychological Distress," *Journal of Rational-Emotive and Cognitive-Behavior Therapy* 14, no. 4 (1996): 265.

[5]Kathy Green, "Psychosocial Factors Affecting Dissertation Completion," *New Directions for Higher Education* 99 (1997): 57-64.

[6]Randy Frost and Deanna Shows, "The Nature and Measurement of Compulsive Indecisiveness," *Behavior Research and Therapy* 31, no. 7 (1993): 691.

[7]Barry Schwartz, *The Paradox of Choice* (New York: HarperCollins, 2004) p. 77.

[8]Ibid., p. 94.

[9]Ibid., pp.128, 148.

[10]Frost and Shows, "Nature and Measurement," p. 691.

[11]Frank Tallis, "Compulsive Washing in the Absence of Phobic and Illness Anxiety," *Behavior Research and Therapy* 34, no. 4 (1996): 361-62. It seems that there are also some people who engage in compulsive washing, not as a result of a strong fear of contamination by germs but from a desire to keep certain things in perfect condition.

[12]A helpful book is by Lee Baer, *The Imp of the Mind: Exploring the Silent Epidemic of Obsessive Bad Thoughts* (New York: Dutton, 2001).

[13]Randy Frost and Gail Steketee, "Perfectionism in Obsessive-Compulsive Disorder Patients," *Behavior Research and Therapy* 35, no. 4 (1997): 291-96.

[14]M. E. McFall and J. P. Wollersheim, "Obsessive-Compulsive Neurosis: A Cognitive-Behavioral

Formulation and Approach to Treatment," *Cognitive Therapy and Research* 3 (1979): 335, quoted in Josee Rheaume et al., "Perfectionism, Responsibility and Obsessive-Compulsive Symptoms," *Behaviour Research and Therapy* 33, no. 7 (1995): 786.

[15]Randy O. Frost and Patricia Marten DiBartolo, "Perfectionism, Anxiety, and Obsessive-Compulsive Disorder," in *Perfectionism: Theory, Research, and Treatment,* ed. Gordon L. Flett and Paul L. Hewitt (Washington, D.C.: American Psychological Association, 2002), p. 361.

[16]*New Catholic Encyclopedia* (New York: McGraw Hill, 1967), s.v. "scrupulosity."

[17]O. Hobart Mowrer, "Transference and Scrupulosity," *Journal of Religion and Health* 2, no. 4 (1963): 329, 331-32.

[18]Gaius Davies, *Genius, Grief and Grace: A Doctor Looks at Suffering and Success* (Fearn, U.K.: Christian Focus Publications, 2003).

[19]David C. Steinmetz, *Luther in Context* (Grand Rapids: Baker Books, 1995), p. 2.

[20]James Kittleston, *Luther the Reformer* (Minneapolis: Augsburg, 1986), p. 287.

[21]Ibid., p. 285.

[22]Davies, *Genius, Grief and Grace*, p. 63.

[23]Ibid., p. 64.

[24]Ibid., p. 60.

Chapter 6: The Thought Patterns of Perfectionism

[1]Paul Tournier, *The Person Reborn* (London: SCM Press, 1967), pp. 86-87.

[2]Joseph Ferrari and William Mautz, "Predicting Perfectionism: Applying Tests of Rigidity," *Journal of Clinical Psychology* 53, no. 1 (1997): 5.

[3]Tournier, *Person Reborn*, p. 86.

[4]Dennis Gibson, "The Obsessive Personality and the Evangelical," *Journal of Psychology and Christianity* 2, no. 3 (1983): 32-33..

[5]Bruce Narramore, "Discipline by Grace," *Journal of Psychology and Theology* 7, no. 4 (1979): 266-67.

[6]Ronald Enroth, *Churches That Abuse,* (Grand Rapids: Zondervan, 1992), p. 29. Ronald Enroth gives many examples of people deeply wounded by legalistic churches. The most extreme abuse and manipulation are seen in the cults that have a strict hierarchy and allow members little freedom to interpret moral principles on their own.

[7]Quoted in William S. Taylor, "Perfectionism in Psychology and in Theology," *Canadian Journal of Theology* 5, no. 3 (1959): 174.

[8]Karen Horney, *Neurosis and Human Growth: The Struggle Toward Self-Realization* (New York: W. W. Norton and Company, 1950), p. 66, quoted in William S. Taylor, "Perfectionism in Psychology and in Theology," *Canadian Journal of Theology* 5, no. 3 (1959): 173.

[9]Peter Slade et al., "An Experimental Analysis of Perfectionism and Dissatisfaction," *The British Journal of Clinical Psychology* 30, no. 2 (1991): 169.

Chapter 7: Genes and Temperament

[1]Gordon Flett et al., "Perfectionism in Children and Their Parents: A Developmental Analysis," in *Perfectionism: Theory, Research, and Treatment,* ed. Gordon L. Flett and Paul L. Hewitt (Washington, D.C.: American Psychological Association, 2002), p. 111.

[2]Kenneth Rice and Karen Preusser, "The Adaptive/Maladaptive Perfectionism Scale," *Measurement and Evaluation in Counseling and Development* 34, no. 4 (2002): 217-18; Kenneth LoCicero, Jeffrey Ashby and Roy Kern, "Multidimensional Perfectionism and Lifestyle Approaches in Middle School Students," *The Journal of Individual Psychology* 56, no. 4 (2000): 449-61;

Paul Hewitt et al., "Perfectionism in Children: Associations with Depression, Anxiety, and Anger," *Personality and Individual Differences* 32, vol. 6 (2002): 1049-61. This research with children aged 10-15 has demonstrated that self-oriented perfectionism is significantly associated with depression and anxiety. Socially prescribed perfectionism is associated with depression, anxiety, social stress, anger and suicide behaviors. There is little research on other-oriented perfectionism at this stage of life.

Chapter 8: Shame and Guilt
[1]Ps 32:1-2; Is 6:7; Heb 10:22

[2]Dick Keyes, *Beyond Identity: Finding Your Way in the Image and Character of God* (Eugene, Ore.: Wipf & Stock, 2003), pp. 32-57.

[3]Anne Lamott, *Bird by Bird: Some Instructions of Writing and Life* (New York: Anchor Books, 1995), p. xvi

[4]Dan Allender, *The Wounded Heart* (Colorado Springs: NavPress, 1990), p. 53.

Chapter 9: Parental Influences
[1]Robert Lenzer, "Disagreements," in *Fathers: A Celebration in Prose, Poetry, and Photography of Fathers and Fatherhood*, ed. Alexandra Towle (New York: Simon & Schuster, 1986), p. 222.

[2]Lewis Paper, "Paternal Guidance," in *Fathers: A Celebration in Prose, Poetry, and Photography of Fathers and Fatherhood*, ed. Alexandra Towle (New York: Simon & Schuster, 1986), p. 162.

[3]Randy Frost and Patricia Marten, "Perfectionism and Evaluative Threat," *Cognitive Therapy and Research* 14, no. 6 (1990): 559-72. This may relate to the early identification between mothers and daughters. In the study, the daughters saw their perfectionist mothers as setting very high standards, being very critical and being very concerned over mistakes. If the daughter saw the mother as particularly "harsh" in her criticism, there was likely to be a greater degree of perfectionism in herself.

[4]Gordon Parker, Hilary Tupling and Laurence B. Brown, "A Parental Bonding Instrument," *British Journal of Medical Psychology* 52 (1979): 1-10.

[5]Jeffrey Ashby, Joseph Mangine and Robert Slaney, "An Investigation of Perfectionism in a University Sample of Adult Children of Alcoholics," *Journal of College Student Development* 36, no. 5 (1995): 452-55. In this study of children of alcoholics, 36 adult children of alcoholics (ACOA) at a university counseling center were compared with 173 students who had not sought counseling and whose parents were not alcoholics. No significant differences were found between the two groups on traits that are seen as positive aspects of perfectionism. However, the ACOA group did show a higher level of maladaptive perfectionism in the form of procrastination, anxiety and problems with relationships. This suggests that having an alcoholic parent is one factor in the formation of unhealthy perfectionism.

[6]Diane H. Baumrind, *Current Patterns of Parental Authority*, Developmental Psychology Monographs, vol. 4, no. 1, part 2 (Washington, D.C.: American Psychological Association, 1971).

[7]Three related studies of perfectionism confirmed that a dispositional tendency to experience shame across a range of situations was reliably linked to socially prescribed perfectionism (SPP). This means that people who feel burdened by unrealistically high standards imposed on them by others are vulnerable to frequent and repeated experiences of shame. In contrast, the other two dimensions of perfectionism—self-oriented (SOP) and other-oriented perfectionism (OOP)—were less associated with shame. The more adaptable and healthy SOPs choose a more realistic task, whereas SPPs, because they have to reach the standards

and goals set by others, often feel their task is impossible and that shame and failure are inevitable (Carol S. Dweck and Ellen L. Leggett, "A Social-Cognitive Approach to Motivation and Personality," *Psychological Review* 95 [1988]: 211-12).

Chapter 10: The Pressures of Culture and Media

[1]Edward Chang, "Cultural Differences, Perfectionism, and Suicidal Risk in a College Population: Does Social Problem Solving Still Matter?" *Cognitive Therapy and Research* 22, vol. 3 (1998): 237-54; Jennifer Castro and Kenneth Rice, "Perfectionism and Ethnicity: Implications for Depressive Symptoms and Self-Reported Academic Achievement," *Cultural Diversity and Ethnic Minority Psychology* 9, no. 1 (2003): 64-78.

[2]"Searching for the Perfect Body," *People Magazine,* September 4, 2000, p. 114-20.

[3]Nancy Franklin, "Keeping Up Appearances," *The New Yorker,* July 28, 2003, p. 93.

[4]Ibid., p. 92

[5]Michael Levine with Hara Estroff Marano, "Why I Hate Beauty," *Psychology Today,* July/August 2001, p. 41.

[6]Alex Kuczynski, "Globe-Hop, but Beware Beauty Lag," *New York Times,* Sunday, April 14, 2002, sec. 9, pp. 1, 6.

[7]Levine and Marano, "Why I Hate Beauty," pp. 41-42.

[8]Ibid.

[9]Karen Hsu, "Figuratively Speaking," *The Boston Globe,* May 20, 1999, B4.

[10]Robin Marantz Henig, "The Price of Perfection," *Civilization* 3, no. 3 (1996): 56-57.

[11]Ibid.

Chapter 11: Anal Fixations and Other Weird and Wonderful Ideas

[1]Leon Salzman, *Treatment of the Obsessive Personality* (New York: Jason Aronson, 1980), pp. 11-12.

[2]Ibid., pp. 8, 12.

[3]Ibid., p. 12.

[4]Alfred Adler, *What Life Should Mean to You* (New York: Blue Ribbon Books, 1931).

[5]Karen Horney, *Neurosis and Human Growth: The Struggle Toward Self-Realization* (New York: W. M. Norton, 1950).

[6]Salzman, *Treatment,* pp. 9, 12-13, 24.

[7]Dennis Gibson, "The Obsessive Personality and the Evangelical," *Journal of Psychology and Christianity* 2, no. 3 (1983): 30.

[8]Joseph Pearce, *Tolkien: Man and Myth* (San Francisco: Ignatius Press, 1998), p. 87.

[9]David Benner, *Psychotherapy and the Spiritual Quest* (Grand Rapids: Baker Books, 1988), p. 142.

Chapter 12: Perfectionism and Pride

[1]There is some empirical evidence of this association. Kenneth Rice and Jacquline Dellwo's recent study of college students found that "perfectionists (adaptive and maladaptive) could be distinguished from non-perfectionists by their higher scores on a measure of grandiosity" ("Perfectionism and Self-Development: Implications for College Adjustment," *Journal of Counseling and Development* 80, no. 2 [2002]: 188-96, quoted in Kenneth Rice and Karen Preusser, "The Adaptive/Maladaptive Perfectionism Scale," *Measurement and Evaluation in Counseling and Development* 34 [2002]: 218). Psychologist June Tangney confirmed the association between pride and other-oriented perfectionism (OOP). She concludes, "It seems that

prideful people feel especially entitled to demand perfection from significant others." In order to feel better about themselves, OOPs often criticize others' failures and do not see their own shortcomings very clearly. Another study linked OOP with narcissism—extreme self-love ("Perfectionism and the Self-Conscious Emotions: Shame, Guilt, Embarrassment, and Pride," in *Perfectionism: Theory, Research and Treatment*, ed. Gordon Flett and Paul Hewitt [Washington, D.C.: American Psychological Association, 2002], pp. 212-13, quoting Paul L. Hewitt, Gordon L. Flett and W. Turnbull, "Perfectionism and Multiphasic Personality Inventory [MMPI] Indices of Personality Disorder," *Journal of Psychopathology and Behavioral Assessment* 14 [1992]: 323-35).

[2]Terry D. Cooper, *Sin, Pride and Self-Acceptance* (Downers Grove, Ill.: InterVarsity Press, 2003), p. 166. This is an excellent exploration of the relationship between low self-esteem and pride.

[3]Dorothy Sayers, *Creed or Chaos? and Other Essays in Popular Theology* (London: The Religious Book Club, 1947), pp. 85-86.

[4]Philip Yancey, *What's so Amazing About Grace?* (Grand Rapids: Zondervan, 1997), p. 45.

[5]R. Larry Shelton in *Evangelical Dictionary of Theology*, ed. Walter A. Elwell, 2nd ed. (Grand Rapids: Baker, 2001), pp. 902-3. I am grateful for the helpful suggestions of a friend and colleague, Old Testament professor Robert Vasholz, who pointed out that, in the Old Testament, sacrificial animals were required to be perfect (*tamim*: "without blemish"), while the requirement for the priests who offered the sacrifices was not such perfection. The priests did, however, have to submit to twelve conditions that made them symbolically "perfect" (Lev 21). This could imply a recognition that no human being could be perfect and is, perhaps, foreshadowing the need for a perfect sacrifice for sin. Christ is described by the apostle Peter as a "lamb without blemish" (1 Pet 1:19).

[6]Reinhold Niebuhr, "The Serenity Prayer."

Chapter 13: Learning to Live with Imperfection

[1]David Burns, "The Perfectionist's Script for Self-Defeat," *Psychology Today*, November 1980, p. 46.

[2]Ibid.

[3]Albert Ellis, "The Role of Irrational Beliefs in Perfectionism," in *Perfectionism: Theory, Research, and Treatment*, ed. Gordon L. Flett and Paul L. Hewitt (Washington, D.C.: American Psychological Association, 2002), pp. 219-20.

[4]Ibid., p. 222.

[5]Martin Antony and Richard Swinson, *When Perfect Isn't Good Enough: Strategies for Coping with Perfectionism* (Oakland, Calif.: New Harbinger, 1998), pp. 124-25. The authors, a psychologist and a psychiatrist, have much experience in helping people with perfectionism, and this is an eminently practical self-help manual. In the first part they cover similar ground to the early part of this book, but in the second part they go into considerable detail on developing a plan for changing perfectionist thoughts and behaviors. In the third part they deal with specific problems such as anger, depression, social anxiety, worry, OCD and body image. However, their discussion of causative factors and cultural influences is very brief, and there is no attempt to include underlying philosophical, religious or spiritual aspects of life.

[6]Benzion Sorotzkin, "Understanding and Treating Perfectionism in Religious Adolescents," *Psychotherapy* 35 (1998): 91, quoted in Gordon Flett and Paul Hewitt, "Perfectionism and Maladjustment: An Overview of Theoretical, Definitional, and Treatment Issues," in *Perfectionism: Theory, Research, and Treatment*, ed. Gordon L. Flett and Paul L. Hewitt (Washington, D.C.: American Psychological Association, 2002), p. 25.

[7]Julia Califano, "The Perils of Perfectionism," *American Health* 15, no. 5 (1996): 72-74.

[8]Antony and Swinson, *When Perfect Isn't Good Enough,* p. 109.

[9]Ibid.

[10]Ibid.

[11]Leon Salzman, *Treatment of the Obsessive Personality* (New York: Jason Aronson, 1980). Salzman goes into great detail in his description of the joys and challenges of working with people who have obsessive and perfectionist personalities.

[12]Ibid., p. 214.

[13]C. S. Lewis, *Mere Christianity* (New York: Macmillan, 1960) p. 154.

Chapter 14: The Search for Identity and Purpose

[1]*The New York Times Magazine*, October 17, 1999, section 6.

[2]Lewis Lapham, "In the Garden Of Tabloid Delight," *Harper's Magazine,* no. 1767 (August 1997): 35

[3]Gertrude Himmelfarb, *The American Scholar*, spring 1997, p. 4. Gertrude Himmelfarb has written extensively on Victorian England and on contemporary society and culture. Her most recent book is *The De-Moralization of Society: From Victorian Virtues to Modern Values* (New York: Vintage Books, 1996).

[4]Charles Darwin, *The Origin of Species by Means of Natural Selection* (New York: The Modern Library, n.d.), p. 529.

[5]*Chariots of Fire* (Burbank: Warner Studios, 1980), film.

[6]A very helpful book on this theme is by Jerram Barrs and Ranald Macauley, *Being Human* (Downers Grove, Ill.: InterVarsity Press, 1978).

[7]Dan Allender and Tremper Longman, *Intimate Allies* (Wheaton, Ill.: Tyndale, 1995), p. 33.

[8]John Stott (address at the National Prayer Breakfast, London, November 22, 1989).

[9]C. S. Lewis, *The Great Divorce* (New York: Macmillan, 1946), pp. 18-21.

[10]Joseph C. Aldrich, *Life-Style Evangelism* (Portland, Ore.: Multnomah, 1981), p. 25.

[11]C. S. Lewis, *Mere Christianity* (New York: Macmillan, 1960), p. 160.

[12]Paraphrase of Romans 12:2 by J. B. Phillips, *Letters to Young Churches: A Translation of the New Testament Epistles* (New York: Macmillan, 1948), p. 27.

Chapter 15: Toward Maturity

[1]Robert Coughlan and the editors of Time-Life Books, *The World of Michelangelo, 1475-1574* (New York: Time, 1966), p. 91.

[2]David Brooks, "The Organization Kid," *The Atlantic Monthly*, April 2001, p. 3.

[3]Ibid., pp. 8-13

[4]Martin Luther, *Works of Martin Luther*, The Philadelphia Edition (Philadelphia: Muhlenberg Press, 1930), 3:31.

[5]Margery Williams Bianco, *The Velveteen Rabbit* (New York: Avon Books, 1975), pp. 16-17.

[6]*Mostly Martha* (Hollywood: Paramount Pictures, 2002), film.

[7]C. S. Lewis, *Mere Christianity* (New York: Macmillan, 1960), p. 161.

Appendix

[1]John Passmore, *The Perfectibility of Man* (London: Gerald Duckworth, 1970), pp. 47-48.

[2]Ibid., p. 67.

[3]Ibid., p. 78.

[4]Ibid., p. 85.

[5]Ibid., p. 71.

[6]David W. Bercot, ed., *A Dictionary of Early Christian Beliefs* (Peabody, Mass.: Hendrickson Publishers, 1998), s.v. "Perfection, Christian" subsection 2.537.

[7]Ibid., p. 75.

[8]Ibid., p. 76.

[9]Ibid., p. 95.

[10]Ibid., p. 121.

[11]Ibid., p. 120.

[12]Ibid., p. 123.

[13]John Calvin, *Insititutes of the Christian Religion,* trans. Ford Lewis Battles, ed. John T. McNeill (Philadelphia: Westminster Press, 1960), 3.6.5.

[14]Ibid., pp. 135-36.

[15]Ibid., p. 136.

[16]Ibid., pp. 138-39.

[17]Ibid., p.141

[18]John R. W. Stott, *Evangelical Truth: A Personal Plea for Unity, Integrity and Faithfulness* (Downers Grove, Ill.: InterVarsity Press, 1999), pp. 98-99.

[19]Benjamin Warfield, in his comprehensive book *Perfectionism* (Philadelphia: Presbyterian and Reformed Publishing, 1974), describes the rise of the Oberlin teaching, the "Higher Life" and the "Victorious Life" movements.

[20]Passmore, *Perfectibility,* p. 142.

[21]Ibid., p. 142.

[22]Ibid., p. 143.

[23]Joseph Smith, "The King Follet Discourse," in *History of the Church of Jesus Christ of Latter-day Saints: An Introduction and Notes by B. H. Roberts,* 2nd ed. (1932-1951; Salt Lake City: Desert Book Company, 1970-1976): 6:306.

[24]Passmore, *Perfectibility,* p. 83.

[25]Reginal Ray, "Mauasiddhas," in *The Encyclopedia of Religion,* ed. Mircea Eliade (New York: Macmillan, 1987), p. 123.

[26]Ibid., p. 124.

[27]Donald Swearer, "Arhat," in *The Encyclopedia of Religion,* ed. Mircea Eliade (New York: Macmillan, 1987), p. 403.

[28]John Lagerway, "Chen-jen," in *The Encyclopedia of Religion,* ed. Mircea Eliade (New York: Macmillan, 1987), pp. 231-33.

[29]Anders Nygren, *The Essence of Christianity: Two Essays* (London: Epworth, 1961), quoted in George Bond, "Perfectibility," in *The Encyclopedia of Religion,* ed. Mircea Eliade (New York: Macmillan, 1987), s.v. "Perfectibility," by George Bond.

[30]Robert Cohn, "Sainthood," in *The Encyclopedia of Religion,* ed. Mircea Eliade (New York: Macmillan, 1987), p. 4.

Names Index

Subject Index